THE SPELLING BEE TOOLBOX™

FOR GRADES 6-8

All the resources you need for a successful Spelling Bee!

by Ann Richmond Fisher

Cover image and design by Bryce A. Fisher

© 2011, 2014 Ann Richmond Fisher

The purchase of this book entitles the buyer to reproduce pages for a single school or home school only. Any other use requires written permission from the author. Contact Ann: spelling.words.well@gmail.com.

All rights reserved.

ISBN-13: 978-0692571118

ISBN-10: 0692571116

THE SPELLING BEE TOOLBOX™
Table of Contents

Introduction	page 4
Instructions	page 5
Rules for Classroom Spelldowns	page 9
Rules for Classroom Spelling Bees	page 10
Rules for All-School Spelling Bees	page 11
Organizational Checklist	page 13
Personnel Chart	page 15
Recorder's Charts	page 16
Audience Guidelines	page 18
Letter to Families	page 19
Sample Press Release	page 20
Classroom Activities and Partner Games	page 21
The Scripps Spelling Bee	page 24
How to Study for a Spelling Bee	page 26
Spelling Rules for Upper Grades	page 28
Study List for Students	page 29
Student Worksheets	page 30
Answers to Worksheets	page 38
Frequently Asked Questions	page 39
620 Spelling Bee Words and Sentences	page 40
Alphabetical Listing of 600 words	page 69
Super Challenge words	page 74
Spelling Bee Clip Art	page 78
Spelling Bee Bookmarks, Reminders & Name Tags	page 79
Deluxe Black and White Award Certificates	page 83
Link to Full-Color Award Certificates	page 101

©Ann Richmond Fisher
The Spelling Bee Toolbox for Grades 6-8

www. spelling-words-well.com

THE SPELLING BEE TOOLBOX ™

Introduction

Dictionary.com defines a Spelling Bee as "a spelling competition won by the individual or team spelling the greatest number of words correctly." Of course, that's true, but a spelling bee is so much more!

A spelling bee motivates students to study spelling words. A spelling bee fosters healthy competition. It recognizes excellence in learning. It brings students into a well-defined structure and requires that they follow rules. And, a spelling bee is FUN!

Spelling bees are growing in popularity worldwide, as shown by the emails, comments and questions I've received from parents, teachers and students around the globe. Folks have requested even more tools than already appear on the website, and they've given me ideas for expanding the ones that are there.

As a result, in this book I've brought together the best tools from the website, all in one place, and I've expanded many of them. Plus, I've added those additional tools that site visitors have requested. You'll find more words, more sentences, more award certificates, more tips for teachers, and so much MORE of everything.

This is the second edition of the Spelling Bee Toolbox, revised and expanded, again based on feedback by website visitors and satisfied customers from around the globe. I've added more helpful resources including the FAQs, personnel chart, audience guidelines, additional certificates, worksheets, name tags, words/sentences and Super Challenge words. In all, I've added more than 20 extra pages.

This Spelling Bee Toolbox is truly the one resource you need for your own successful spelling bees!

Thanks for your support of www.spelling-words-well.com. Please keep the comments coming.

Ann
ann@spelling-words-well.com

THE SPELLING BEE TOOLBOX™
Instructions

In order to gain the maximum benefit from the tools in this eBook, please refer to these instructions for each section of manual.

Guidelines for Three Kinds of Spelling Bees
The set of rules you choose to follow will depend on:
- The setting of your spelling bee
- The number of spellers who are participating
- The number of people involved in conducting the bee
- The time that's available for the bee

I recommend you read through the guidelines for all the types of bees listed here, and then pick and choose the features that will work best for your situation. Once you've decided on the rules you'll use, be certain to make the rules clear to all the students, parents and teachers who will be involved in the activity. Then be sure to follow the rules consistently during the contest.

Organizing a Spelling Bee
Use this checklist to get organized and stay organized. Adjust the list as needed for your situation. If you are responsible for a large bee, please don't ignore this tool!

Personnel Chart
Here's a place to record everyone's name and phone number who is involved in your big bee. You may not need to fill every position, and you may need to add some that are not listed. Once you've filled out this page, make copies for others as needed.

Recorder's Chart
The recorder (or one of the judges) can use this helpful tool to keep track of which spellers are in and out of the competition. It's important to note the round on which each one is eliminated, the misspelled word, and the misspelling in case of disputes later. The first page is numbered for the first twenty students in the first 8 rounds. The second page can be photocopied as needed for subsequent rounds and additional spellers.

Audience Guidelines
Include some or all of these in your printed programs, or ask your emcee to read them at the beginning of any major spelling bee. Don't let unnecessary distractions upset your spellers! Be sure to cover #4 with your judges. Use it only with their agreement.

Family Letter
Use this letter as is, or adapt for your situation. It's essential to communicate early and often with families. You can also adapt this for email and Facebook posts.

Press Release
Members of the press won't know about your event unless you tell them! Use this format to formally announce your Bee to local newspapers, radio and television stations. Be sure to include the *who, what, where, when* info at the very beginning of your press release. Reporters love a good local story, so be sure to include interesting details about your bee that will draw their attention and make them *want* to promote your event!

Classroom Activities and Partner Game
Use these ideas to help students gain confidence in spelling in front of others and to increase their spelling proficiency. These ideas can be used year-round, even when your students are *not* participating in a spelling bee.

The Scripps Spelling Bee
This information answers some basic questions about the world's most famous bee. Use the links to learn more.

How to Study for a Spelling Bee
Give students this helpful guide as early as possible. Review the suggestions frequently in class.

Spelling Rules for Upper Grades
This list includes a few of the well-known spelling rules that, hopefully, most upper grade students have mastered. It also contains some of the more obscure ones that may help students spell some tricky words correctly.

Study List
These 100 words are a good sampling of words students might expect to encounter in any spelling bee. Approximately 70 of these words appear in the mega-list of 600 words in this eBook.

Worksheets
Use these formats to make more of your own worksheets using new words. Better yet, ask your *students* to create the worksheets to share with classmates. The more times students use their spelling words, the more likely they are to remember them.

Frequently Asked Questions
This brief sections covers some key points about the big word lists and study lists for students that I'm often asked. It's worth a few minutes of your time.

Spelling Bee Words and Sentences
Our list of 620 words was gleaned from a variety of grade-level resources. Many of the words appear in the spelling bee word lists on our website. Be sure to read through the words in advance of any spelling bee to rearrange, add and omit words as you see fit.

Also read through all the sentences prior to your competition. **Feel free to use your own sentences for any of the ones here that you feel are not meaningful or appropriate for your students.** Sentences are purposely brief. Many sentences give clues to the words' meanings as an aid to the speller. You don't need to use every word on the list. Skip over any words that you think might cause problems.

In general, our words appear from easiest to most difficult. However, this will not always be true for every speller. There are about 20 5th grade words included near the beginning of the list. There are many words at the 9th grade level and beyond toward the end of the list.

You may start with any word on the list, depending on the level of your students. Here are some general guidelines:
Grade 6 – Start at the beginning
Grade 7 – Start around #150
Grade 8 – Start around #300

During the bee, you may choose to skip large sections of the list in order to get to more difficult words more quickly.

Alphabetical Listing of 620 Spelling Bee Words
This quick reference tool will allow you to compare our word list to your own spelling curriculum and other resources.

Super Challenge List
Use these words to challenge your best spellers or to supplement our list of 620 words during your spelling bee. Throughout the school year, be on the lookout for more super-challenge words to add to this list.

Clip art
Use these images to spruce up your flyers and letters. Here's one way to use our clip art as digital images:
1. Scroll to the page(s) with the image(s) you wish to use.
2. Press the "print screen" button on your keyboard.
3. Open up a new document in "Paint" or other image-editing program of your choice.
4. Insert the image from "print screen" by using Ctl + V or "insert"
5. Crop the image(s) you want. Resize as necessary.
6. In the file menu, click on "Save as." Name the file, save as a .jpg or .png in your documents or picture files in a location you can find later.
7. Open up a word document, then Insert --> Picture --> from file. Go to the saved location of your clip art image.
8. Adjust the image size as necessary as well as its layout properties. Complete your letter, announcement or other document.

Bookmarks
Photocopy these designs on card stock, cut apart and laminate.

Reminders
Use these for students, their families, and even spelling bee officials.

Name Tags
Photocopy enough to have one per student . Write in students' names and grade or other ID information and laminate, if desired. Cut out. Punch holes in upper corners and add string or yarn so that name tags can be hung around students' necks, as shown.

Award Certificates
Choose the awards that best fit the mood of your competition – serious, fun, modern, or traditional – in either color or black and white. You can follow either of these procedures in presenting the awards:
1) Print out the certificates of your choice prior to your spelling bee. After the bee, write in the winners' names and present them immediately or at a later date.
2) After the bee, open the certificates of your choice in a pdf-editing program. Insert the winners' names and print. Present the awards at a later ceremony.

THE SPELLING BEE TOOLBOX ™
Classroom Spelldown

This is a great format to use in your classroom in a single class period. The "team spirit" factor helps spellers encourage one another. Misspelled words are spelled again and again until they're corrected, making this a valuable instructional tool.

1. Divide students into two teams.

2. Each team lines up on opposite sides of the room, facing each other.

3. The teacher reads the first word to Player 1 on Team A. She also uses the word in a sentence.

4. Player 1 repeats the word, spells it, and says the word again.

5. If the player is correct, he moves to the end of the line on team A. The teacher gives the next word to the first player on Team B.

6. If the player is incorrect, the player sits down and is out of the spelldown. The teacher gives the same word to player 1 on Team B.

7. Player 1 on Team B repeats the word, spells it, and says the word again.

8. If she is correct, she moves to the end of the line on her team.

9. The Spelldown continues with correct players moving to the end of the line, and incorrect players leaving the competition. Eventually, the students who have spelled correctly will move to the front of the line to spell again and again. At some point, one team will have only one speller. That student must spell every time it's his team's turn.

10. The spelldown ends when one team has lost all its spellers. The winning team is the one with the last speller(s) standing.

Variation:
If the same word is misspelled by two (or choose a different number) players, both players *remain in the spelldown*. The teacher writes the correct spelling of the missed word on the board and gives those players a new word to spell.

THE SPELLING BEE TOOLBOX™
Classroom Spelling Bee

This individual competition is slightly more competitive than the spelldown, but not as rigid as the formal spelling bee, outlined below.

1. Determine the order in which students will spell. Arrange spellers in that order in their seats or in an open area of the classroom.

2. The teacher announces the word to be spelled. He speaks slowly and clearly, without distorting the normal pronunciation of the word. He uses the word in a sentence and says the word again.

3. The speller listens carefully to the teacher and asks for the word to be repeated if necessary.

4. When the speller is sure she understands the word, she pronounces it, spells it and then says the word again.

5. The teacher determines whether or not the word was spelled correctly.

6. If the correct spelling was given, the speller remains in the bee.

7. If the spelling was incorrect, that speller is eliminated from the bee. The teacher gives the correct spelling of that word. Then the teacher reads a new word to the next student.

8. The bee continues until all but two spellers have been eliminated. When there are only two spellers left, if one player misspells a word, the other player must spell that word correctly, plus one more word to be declared the winner of the spelling bee.

THE SPELLING BEE TOOLBOX ™
All-School (or Large) Spelling Bee

For this type of spelling bee, you'll need several officials: a pronouncer, at least one judge, a recorder and, optionally, a timekeeper. See list on page 15.

The spelling bee coordinator should select officials for these positions who speak clearly, listen carefully and who will follow the guidelines you present to them.

Advance preparation by the spelling bee officials:

Judges
Read the rules and the word list. Select and secure a large dictionary to use on the day of the bee. Designate one person as the head judge who will make the final decisions on the correct or incorrect spelling of a word.

Pronouncer
Read through the word list in advance. Look up the correct pronunciation of any unfamiliar words in a dictionary. Learn the rules for the bee.

Recorder
Read the rules and word list in advance. Review the recorder's chart.

Timekeeper-Optional (See rule 4B)
During the bee, the timekeeper uses a stopwatch to keep track of the amount of time the speller uses to complete the spelling of each word. The time limit must be decided in advance and announced to all participants. A limit of 30 - 60 seconds is recommended, depending on the age of the students, the difficulty of the words, and the available time for the bee.

Spelling bee coordinator
Be sure to meet with the spelling bee officials prior to the bee to make sure all the rules and procedures are clear.

Immediately before the bee begins:

(For a more complete checklist, see page 13.)

1. Decide the order in which the students will participate. Seat them in order on stage, or at the front of the room.

2. Arrange a table for the judges and recorder.

3. Be sure all members of the audience are seated and quiet.

To conduct the bee, the head judge reads the rules and procedures aloud to the spellers and audience. He asks the spellers if they have any questions about the rules.

Rules:

1. The first speller goes to the microphone.

2. The pronouncer announces the word to be spelled. He speaks slowly and clearly, without distorting the normal pronunciation of the word. He uses the word in a sentence and says the word again.

3. The speller listens carefully to the pronouncer and asks for the word to be repeated if necessary.

4. When the speller is sure she understands the word, she pronounces it, spells it and then says the word again. She must say it loudly enough for the judge(s) to hear it.

Optional additions to this rule:
    A. Once a speller has started spelling the word, she may start over as long as she has not finished spelling the word and repeated it. **OR**
    Once a speller has started to spell the word, she may not start over.

    B. Spellers will have a time limit of ___ seconds in which to complete the spelling of the word, from the time she indicates to the pronouncer that she understands the word she is to spell.

5. The judge(s) determines whether or not the word was spelled correctly.

6. If the correct spelling was given, the speller remains in the bee and goes back to her seat.

7. If the spelling was incorrect, that speller is eliminated from bee. The speller leaves the stage at the end of the round, i.e. after each speller has taken one turn. (Optional variations: The speller leaves the stage immediately.)

8. If the word was misspelled, the judge gives the correct spelling of that word. Then the pronouncer reads a new word to the next student.

9. This process continues with correct spellers staying in the competition and incorrect spellers being eliminated.

10. When there are only two spellers left, if one player misspells a word, the other player must spell that word correctly, plus one more word to be declared the winner of the spelling bee.

THE SPELLING BEE TOOLBOX™
Organizational Checklist

Use this checklist to plan a school-wide or district-wide spelling bee. Check off each task as it is completed.

6-12 months in advance
- ☐ Form a group of 3-4 people to help organize the spelling bee.
- ☐ Decide what schools, grades or ages will compete in your spelling bee.
- ☐ Set the date.
- ☐ Reserve the facilities you will need.
- ☐ Notify teachers, students, parents, and administrators of the date of the bee and the eligibility requirements.
- ☐ Discuss the funds that will be needed for the event. Learn what resources are already available and how much more money you may need to raise.
- ☐ Contact local businesses, if necessary, to help fund your event.

3-6 months in advance
- ☐ Decide what word lists you will use. Let spellers know in advance. We recommend the list of 620 words in this book. But you may decide to make your own list based on your own spelling curriculum. The Scripps National Spelling Bee uses *Webster's Third New International Dictionary* and its Addenda Section (copyright 2002 by Merriam-Webster), which means those spellers must be ready for anything! Whatever you decide, be sure that students have at least some of the words in advance and/or know what dictionary you'll be using.
- ☐ Choose your Spelling Bee pronouncer, judges, record keeper, and timekeeper, if needed. Double-check their availability for your date.
- ☐ Double-check on the availability of your facility.
- ☐ If your bee will be held at a location other than your own school, arrange to have someone attend your event that is familiar with the building. Be sure you have someone to run the sound system.
- ☐ Decide on the spelling bee rules you will use. (See page 11 for our suggestions.) Send written copies to students, parents, teachers, and all bee officials.
- ☐ Decide if you want to serve refreshments and if so, what type of foods and beverages you want to include. Then find a very responsible person to be in charge of that portion of the event.

1-2 months in advance
- Decide on prizes. Choose award certificates included in this book, or order medals and trophies from local vendors or online sources. (Allow at least 6 weeks for special orders.)
- Check back with all participants frequently. One month before the spelling bee, send a note to all classrooms and bee officials reminding them of the date. Tell them what time they should arrive at the competition.
- Get a list of the names of all students who expect to participate.
- Notify local newspapers, radio stations, and TV stations to let them know about the spelling bee. See the Sample Press Release on page 20.
- Invite sponsors to attend.

1-2 weeks in advance
- Announce the bee on your Face Book page and other social media.
- If you're using a stage, be sure you have chairs, a podium, microphones, and tables for the judges.
- Make name tags for all participants and officials.
- Print out word lists for the pronouncers and judges. Print the recorder's chart (pages 16-17) for the record keeper. Gather dictionaries, pencils, and a stopwatch.
- Contact media personnel again and encourage them to cover your big event.

The day of the Spelling Bee
- Arrive 2 hours early with you word lists, dictionaries, recorder's charts, pencils, awards and name tags.
- Check the sound system and seating.
- Welcome your spellers, staff and audience.
- Publicly thank sponsors, spellers, teachers, parents, staff and media.
- *Enjoy the bee!*

After the Spelling Bee
- Clean up the facility, if necessary.
- Announce the spelling bee winners in public forums.
- Send a thank you note to everyone who helped with the bee.
- Recover and start planning for next year!

THE SPELLING BEE TOOLBOX™
Personnel

	Name	Phone number/Email address
Coordinator	_____	_____
Central Planning Team	_____	_____
	_____	_____
	_____	_____
	_____	_____
Emcee	_____	_____
Judge (s)	_____	_____
	_____	_____
Pronouncer	_____	_____
Recorder	_____	_____
Timekeeper	_____	_____
Sound technician	_____	_____
Facilities manager	_____	_____
Publicity coordinator	_____	_____
_____	_____	_____
_____	_____	_____
_____	_____	_____

THE SPELLING BEE TOOLBOX™
Recorder's Chart

Student	Round								Misspelled Word
	1	2	3	4	5	6	7	8	
Example: Tim Smith	✓	✓	✓	✓	X				sincerly
1.									
2.									
3.									
4.									
5.									
6.									
7.									
8.									
9.									
10.									
11.									
12.									
13.									
14.									
15.									
16.									
17.									
18.									
19.									
20.									

©Ann Richmond Fisher
The Spelling Bee Toolbox for Grades 6-8

www. spelling-words-well.com

THE SPELLING BEE TOOLBOX™
Recorder's Chart – Additional pages

Student	Round								Misspelled Word

THE SPELLING BEE TOOLBOX™
Audience Guidelines

Thank you for attending our spelling bee. Your support means so much to our spellers! In order to help them concentrate and perform at their very best, please observe these guidelines:

1. During each round, remain quiet and in your seat.

2. If you must leave your seat, please wait until the end of a round to leave the room. Also wait until the end of a round to reenter the room.

3. Do not spell any word aloud. Do not even whisper it to yourself or to your neighbor.

4. Do not argue with the judges. Their decisions are final. If you feel strongly that a mistake was made, please write down what you observed.

At the end of that round, ask the judges for a moment of their time. It is their option to receive your comment or not, and to act upon it, or not. Again, their decisions are final.

5. Hold your applause until the end of the spelling bee, as instructed by the spelling bee officials.

It's Spelling Bee Time!

Dear Families,

A very important event involving your student is coming up! Please mark this information on your calendar now.

      The _____ Spelling Bee

Date:

Time:

Location:

Here are several ways you can help your student prepare for the Bee:

1) Help your student study spelling words frequently. Ask him/her to spell them aloud. You can study word lists that I will be sending home, words from other textbooks, words from the newspaper and unfamiliar words from the dictionary.

2) On the week of the Spelling Bee, and especially the night before the Bee, make sure your student gets plenty of rest and proper nutrition.

3) If at all possible, plan to attend the Bee. If you are unable to attend, please try to arrange for another family member or friend to be there. Your presence will be a huge encouragement to *all* of our students.

If I can be of further assistance, please contact me at:_____

Thank you in advance for your support!

Sincerely,

Sample Press Release

Wilson Middle School
123 Scholarly Drive
Lansing, MI 49ZIP
(123) 456-7890

FOR IMMEDIATE RELEASE　　　　　　**Contact:** John Doe, Spelling Bee Coordinator
(123) 456-7890 x987

10th Annual Wilson Middle School Spelling Bee – November 9

Lansing, MI – On Tuesday, November 9, at 10 A.M, the Wilson Middle School will hold its tenth annual spelling bee competition in the school's auditorium. Admission is free and open to the public.

Twenty-four students from grades 6, 7, and 8 will compete for the title of school champion. The champion will represent the school next month in the Ingham County Spelling Bee.

Mayor Sue Jones will be on hand to present the trophy to this year's winner. The winner will also receive a $100 U.S. Savings Bond, compliments of Acme Services, this year's sponsor.

School principal, Ms. Sondra Smith, notes that two past winners of Wilson Middle Spelling Bee have gone on to compete at the state and national levels. She urges the public to attend the event and encourage the hard-working students.

Each participant has already competed at his/her own grade level and finished among the top 8 in his/her class. During the all-school competition, participants will be asked to spell words from lists they have not previewed. It should prove to be a challenging competition for all students.

For more information about the Wilson Middle School Spelling Bee, please contact *John Doe at 123.456.7890.987 or j.doe@email.address.*

THE SPELLING BEE TOOLBOX™
Classroom Activities

You can help your students prepare for spelling bees all year long. Their success in spelling bees will depend on two factors:
A) Spelling proficiency
B) Confidence spelling aloud in front of others

To help students gain proficiency in their spelling skills:

1) Challenge students each week with a few tough words. Write the words on the board at the beginning of each week and discuss their meanings. Include these difficult words on the weekly spelling quiz and in other written assignments. Use words from the list of spelling bee words at then end of this book, from word lists at www.spelling-words-well.com and/or from the dictionary.

2) Ask students to contribute the challenge words. Assign a different pair of students each week to find 5 difficult words. At the beginning of each week, the pair can do a brief oral presentation in which they write the words on the board and explain their meaning.

3) Review common spelling rules with students. See pages 28-29.

4) Give students extra written practice with difficult words. Reading and writing are essential experiences, especially for visual learners.

5) Frequently review commonly misspelled words such as *separate, occasionally, achieve,* and *definitely.*

To help students gain confidence in spelling aloud:

1) Conduct frequent, brief oral quizzes. At the beginning or end of a class period, use just a minute or two for "popcorn" quizzes. Randomly call out a student's name and a spelling word. For example, say "Rachel, *organize.*" Rachel pops up and spells organize. If she's incorrect, call on the student seated behind her, "Ali, *organize.*," and so on. This not only gives frequent practice, it motivates students to study the weekly spelling words.

2) Ask students to do oral reading, oral math, or any kind of oral presentation from their seats and especially in front of the class.

For a fun change, try the partner game on the next two pages. It can be played over and over with new words every time!

Can You Spell It?

Players must pay close attention to the letter diagram as they try to spell words in this challenging game. Use a new board every time for maximum usefulness!

Object of the game: Correctly locate and spell the most words

Supplies: Game board, list of spelling words, paper and pencil, 15 blank index cards

Preparation: Write one spelling word on each index card. Shuffle the word cards and place them face down on the table. Write a letter in each space in the game board. (Use letters that are in the set of spelling words.) Each player numbers his paper from 1 to 15 and makes two columns on his paper. He writes YES at the top of one column and NO at the top of the other.

To Play:

1. The first player draws a word card and reads it aloud.

2. Both players look carefully at the game board. Each one silently decides if the word can be spelled by moving from letter to letter following the lines on the board.

3. Each player writes the spelling word under the correct column on his paper. He writes the word under YES if he can spell it, and under NO if he cannot. See example below.

4. The second player draws a word card and reads it aloud. Play continues until all the cards have been drawn.

5. At the end of the game, players compare their answers. They check to be sure the other player has spelled each word correctly on his/her paper, and that he/she has placed it in the correct column. If players answers differ, they work together to find the right answer.

6. The winner of the game is the player with the most answers spelled correctly and placed under the correct column.

Example:

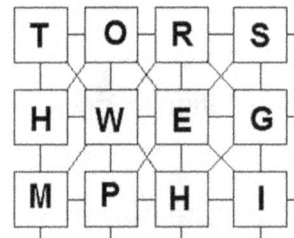

	Yes	No
1.	two	
2.		whisper
3.		whom
4.	weigh	

from *AnyWord™ Partner Activities,* © 2012 Ann Richmond Fisher
www.spelling-words-well.com/anyword-spelling-worksheets-ebooks.html

Can You Spell It?
Game Board

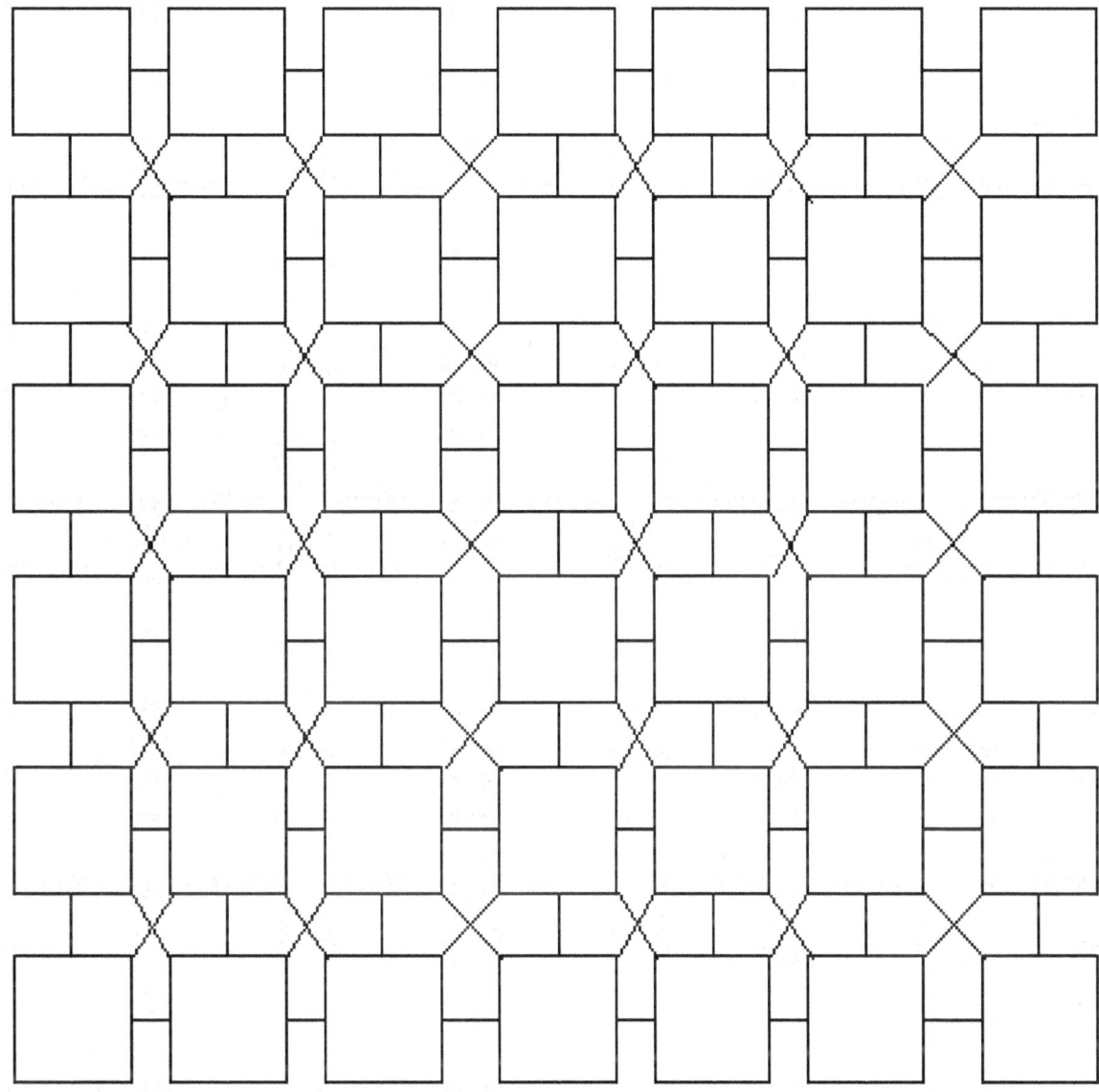

from **AnyWord™ Partner Activities,** © 2012 Ann Richmond Fisher
www.spelling-words-well.com/anyword-spelling-worksheets-ebooks.html

The Scripps Spelling Bee

No spelling bee resource would be complete without mentioning the Scripps Spelling Bee, the oldest national spelling competition in the United States. It began in 1925 and is run as a not-for-profit competition by the E.W. Scripps Company. It is the "bee of all spelling bees" with final rounds aired on television stations around the world.

Eligibility
In order to be eligible to compete in the Scripps National Spelling Bee, students must attend a school that is enrolled in the Scripps program. (See Scripps FAQs for rules regarding homeschooled students.) Students must be under the age of 16 and in grades 8 or below.

Schools must follow certain rules and pay an enrollment fee to participate in Scripps. Local businesses (often newspapers) pay the fee and become sponsors of the bee. Schools must enroll with the national office from mid-August through mid-October.

Participating schools are located in the U.S., Canada, Puerto Rico, New Zealand, South Korea, U.S. Department of Defense schools in Europe, and several other locations.

The Process
While different regions follow different plans, usually schools hold several small competitions. For example, each classroom might hold its own bee. Then the winners from each classroom might compete against each other in school wide spelling bee. Next, the winners from several schools in the same city or county might compete against each other. Regional and statewide competitions may also follow.

Normally, champions compete at several levels before moving on to the finals which are held at the Grand Hyatt Hotel in Washington, D.C. The finals are always held during the week following Memorial Day.

Preparation
Students who are serious about competing in the Scripps competition study all year long, for hours every day. Students in enrolled schools can receive lists of words to study from Scripps. Merriam-Webster also provides study helps. In addition to learning the spellings of words, it is also very helpful students to learn definitions, pronunciations, parts of speech and etymologies of words.

Many champion students study straight from the *Third New International Dictionary of the English Language,* the official dictionary used by Scripps. They also read good books to learn new words. They often keep a special list of their own interesting words to memorize.

Prizes
The champion of the annual Scripps National Spelling Bee receives:
- $30,000 cash
- a huge engraved trophy called a loving cup
- reference books from Merriam-Webster and Encylopaedia Britannica
- other monetary prizes.

All spellers who make it to the finals receive prizes, based on the number of rounds they successfully complete.

Students who participate in any of the spelling bees are rewarded with the experience of being part of a fun, educational competition. They also enjoy the benefits of learning new words and expanding their vocabularies.

Helpful links:

Home page for the Scripps Spelling Bee: http://www.spellingbee.com/

School enrollment page for Scripps: https://secure.spellingbee.com/enrollment/register

Complete student eligibility rules: http://www.spellingbee.com/eligibility

FAQs for Scripps: http://www.spellingbee.com/customer-service-center

List of past champions and their winning words:
http://www.spellingbee.com/champions-and-their-winning-words

THE SPELLING BEE TOOLBOX ™
How to Study for a Spelling Bee

In a weekly spelling quiz, you know exactly which words you'll be asked to spell. But in a spelling bee, you could be asked to spell just about anything! So what's the best way to prepare to spell well at your next competition?

There are several strategies you should use. Some are long-term practices, and others can be used at the last minute to boost your skills.

Long term - What you should do all year long

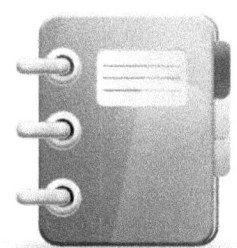

1. Maintain a spelling notebook. This can be a pocket-sized tablet or a large spiral-bound pad. Write down words that are tricky for you – words you've misspelled on spelling quizzes or writing assignments. Also write down words you encounter that you don't know how to spell very well. Review the words in your notebook frequently.

2. Read a lot to expand your vocabulary. Your reading should include good books and the newspaper. You'll learn new words and how to use them. Add the most interesting words and the ones with the trickiest spellings in your spelling notebook.

3. Be sure to master the spelling words you're given in language class each week, as well as vocabulary words from science, social studies and math classes.

4. Practice difficult words over and over. Write them on paper, and type them into a text document. This repetition helps you see and spell and cement the words in your memory.

5. Discover your best "on stage" spelling bee method. Think about how you prepare to spell a word aloud. Are you most successful if you
- trace it with your finger
- say it to yourself
- or picture it in your mind?

Figure this out in advance. Then once a week, have a friend or family member ask you to spell a few words aloud, spelling bee style. Get comfortable with spelling tricky words in front of other people.

6. Learn basic spelling strategies and rules. (See page 28.) In your notebook, make a list of commonly-used words that are exceptions to these rules.

7. If you're really serious about advancing to regional, state or national competitions, you need to get a good dictionary and study it. *Webster's New International Dictionary of the English Language, Unabridged* is the largest dictionary of the English language, with over 450,000 entries. It's the one used by the Scripps' National Spelling Bee, making it the perfect one to study for advanced spelling bee competitions.

8. Talk to other students who have done well in spelling bees. Talk to older students, your brothers or sisters, or classmates who have done well. What tips worked for them? You can also read books about successful spellers, including *How to Spell Like a Champ* by Trinkle, Andrews and Kimble.

Short term - What you can do weeks or days before the spelling bee

1. Ask your teacher for specific list of words you can study. Then study! See the word lists at www.spelling-words-well.com if you need more words to study.

2. Practice spelling a lot of words aloud with a friend or family member.

3. Post spelling words everywhere: the bathroom mirror, your computer desktop, your school desk or locker. Carry a list of words you want to learn in your pocket. Pull out the list and study it when you have spare minutes between other activities.

4. Ask someone to quiz you on words that you haven't studied before. A good place to find words is on the front page of a newspaper.

5. Review the tips in the long-term list above and work on them as much as possible.

6. The night before the spelling bee, get plenty of rest. Eat a good breakfast in the morning. Include some protein, such as eggs, cheese or peanut butter.

7. Most importantly, believe you can do it! Your preparation will give you confidence to think clearly and spell correctly, despite the butterflies in your stomach.

THE SPELLING BEE TOOLBOX™
Spelling Rules for Upper Grades

By now you probably know the basic spelling rules, such as when to change a final *y* to *i* when forming plurals and whether or not to double consonants when adding suffixes. It's a good idea to review those rules prior to any competition, and also to review words that are exceptions to those rules.

There are also some lesser-used rules that are worth reviewing. These rules may help you figure out how to spell unfamiliar words that you may encounter in a spelling bee. We'll take a look at 12 rules (of both types) here.

1. Compound Words
Keep both words whole. Don't drop the last letter of the first word or the first letter of the last word. Examples: roommate, bookkeeper, sidewalk, withhold.

2. Words spelled with *ie* or *ei*
Use *i* before *e* except after *c* or when sounded like *a* as in *neighbor* and *weigh*. Examples: friend, believe, ceiling, receive, eight, vein Note: There are many exceptions to this rule, including: *neither, science, their, weird, ancient, height, protein, sufficient* and more. These words need to be memorized.

Forming Plurals

3. Words that end in *y*
A) If a noun ends in a consonant followed by a *y*, change the *y* to *i* and add *es*.
Examples: candies, stories

B) If a noun ends in a vowel followed by a *y*, add *s*.
Examples: chimneys, turkeys

4. Words that end in *f or fe*
Most nouns ending in *f* or *fe* form the plural by changing the *f* or *fe* to *v* and adding -*es*. For a double *f*, just add *s*. Examples: calves, wives, knives, bluffs, cliffs, hooves.
Exception: roofs

5. Making plurals from words that end in *o*
A) If a vowel comes before the final o, add s. Examples: radios, studios

B) If a consonant comes before the final o, usually add es. Examples: potatoes, echoes

The plural forms of *mosquito* and *tornado* can be spelled either way.

Interesting note: The plural of most words related to music that end in *o* are formed by adding *s* only. Examples: solos, pianos

Adding Prefixes

6. When adding prefixes such as *dis- mis-, pre- re-, un,* the spelling of the base word does not change.
Examples: disability, misspell, preamble, react, unusual.

Adding Suffixes

7. Words that end in *e*
A) Drop the *e* when the suffix begins with a vowel. (-ed, -ing, -ous, -able, –y)
Examples: closed, housing, nervous, adorable, lousy
Exceptions: noticeable, courageous
A few words can be spelled either way: loveable or lovable, movable or moveable.

B) Keep the silent *e* when the suffix begins with a consonant (-ment, -ful, -ly)
Example: careful, movement
Exceptions: ninth, truly
Judgment and *acknowledgment* are preferred spellings; however, *judgement* and *acknowledgement* are accepted.

8. Doubling the final consonant
If a one-syllable word ends with a vowel followed by a consonant, double the consonant before adding the suffix. Examples: stopping, bedding, dipper

Note that words like *read* become *reading* because there are two vowels before the final consonant. Words like *helping* have one *p* because they end in two consonants.

9. Adding *-less*
When adding *–less*, the base word does not usually change. Examples: hopeless, clueless.

10. Adding *-ful*
The suffix *–ful* never has two ls. When *–ful* is added to a word, the spelling of the base word usually does not change. Examples: soulful, cheerful, careful.

11. Adding *–able* and *–ible*
A) If the base word is whole, the suffix is usually spelled *-able*. The silent *e* is dropped before adding this suffix. Examples: breakable, acceptable, lovable, believable

B) If the base word is incomplete or is a root, the suffix is usually spelled *-ible*. Examples: divisible, possible, terrible.

12. Words that end in *c*
When *c* is the last letter of a word, it is always hard. When adding the suffixes *–er,–ing,* or *–y,* first add a *k* to keep the hard *c* sound. Examples: picnicker, panicky, trafficking.

THE SPELLING BEE TOOLBOX™
Study List for Students

Here are 100 words to learn before your next spelling bee.

1. absurd
2. accompaniment
3. acknowledgement
4. amateur
5. anonymous
6. anxious
7. archeology
8. arraign
9. asphalt
10. attendance
11. auxiliary
12. bankruptcy
13. barracuda
14. bizarre
15. broccoli
16. callous
17. cease
18. chasm
19. chlorophyll
20. clique
21. colonel
22. condominium
23. conscientious
24. corroborate
25. croissant
26. culprit
27. democracy
28. dialogue
29. diligent
30. dismissal
31. dulcimer
32. echoes
33. eczema
34. embargo
35. etiquette
36. exaggeration
37. facsimile
38. fatigue
39. finesse
40. fracas
41. frugal
42. gauge
43. grotesque
44. haphazard
45. haughty
46. hindrance
47. hurriedly
48. hypotenuse
49. hypothesis
50. inaugural
51. incessant
52. incisor
53. influential
54. infrastructure
55. interrogate
56. jewelry
57. khaki
58. laborious
59. lieutenant
60. miniature
61. miscellaneous
62. negligible
63. novice
64. nuisance
65. occasionally
66. opulent
67. orator
68. outrageous
69. parliament
70. percent
71. plasma
72. predecessor
73. prosperity
74. pseudonym
75. qualm
76. quandary
77. recipe
78. reciprocal
79. remembrance
80. rhythmic
81. sabotage
82. schism
83. secretary
84. solemn
85. spontaneous
86. subsequent
87. succinct
88. superfluous
89. surveillance
90. technically
91. tomatoes
92. unanimous
93. unenforceable
94. vaccinate
95. vegetable
96. vicious
97. vivacious
98. vulnerable
99. wholly
100. withhold

©Ann Richmond Fisher
The Spelling Bee Toolbox for Grades 6-8

TOUGH CHOICE

You'll need to make two correct decisions for each word on this page. First, choose the correct spelling of each word. Then write the correct spellings in the sentences below so that each sentence makes sense. You will use two of the words more than once.

contagious/contagous   preferable/preferrable
disasterous/disastrous   recyclable/recycleable
familar/familiar   sincerely/sincerly
feirce/fierce   spaceous/spacious
foreign/foriegn   unmistakable/unmistakeable

1. The luxury car was especially _____ on the inside.

2. It is _____ that you work correctly rather than quickly.

3. The _____ wind blew loudly, making it difficult to fall asleep.

4. Because the disease was very _____, many people in the village became ill.

5. The _____ currency is worth more today than the U.S. dollar.

6. I _____ hope my thoughtless remark did not offend you.

7. He looks _____, but I can't remember where I've seen him before.

8. The _____ aroma of Mom's spaghetti sauce greeted me as I walked in the door.

9. When the puppy jumped onto the shelf of fine china, the results were _____.

10. Please keep your _____ waste in a separate trash can.

11. Her laughter was so _____ that soon everyone in the room was laughing with her.

12. Because the competition was so _____, only the very best players succeeded.

ORDER, PLEASE!

Write this list of tricky spelling words in alphabetical order. Then write the words again in reverse alphabetical order.

1. ancient
2. acquaintance
3. accept
4. amnesty
5. apostrophe
6. accidentally
7. appreciate
8. achievement
9. ability
10. aerial
11. accelerate
12. appearance
13. analysis
14. ambassador
15. apparatus
16. acquittal
17. ancestor
18. accommodate
19. abstain
20. accessible

FIT FOR FOUR

Fit each four-letter word into the blanks in the longer words below, one letter at a time to complete a common word. You should be able to match the words so that you use each four-letter word exactly once.

Example: __ o p u __ __ r i t __   Insert the word *play* to spell *popularity*.

Words to insert:			
arid	neat	pare	toes
been	noon	pole	tree
gale	note	poor	vain
hill	only	rule	veil
meat	pale	teal	wand

1. __ __ g o t i __ __ e

2. s u r __ __ __ l __ a n c e

3. t e c __ n __ c a __ __ y

4. u __ d __ u b __ __ d l y

5. v __ __ __ e g a t e __

6. __ r __ p e l __ __ r

7. __ r d i __ a r i __ __

8. s o __ h __ m __ __ e

9. p h e __ __ __ m e n __ __

10. __ __ r a __ l __ l

11. v e __ e t __ b __ __ __

12. p o __ __ n t i __ __

13. __ __ m a t o __ __

14. __ __ c c __ __ a t e

15. r e __ __ i __ v __

16. s e __ __ __ __ a t __ l y

17. n e __ s s t __ __ __

18. o __ __ d i __ __ t

19. n u __ __ r __ __ o r

20. t u __ b __ __ __ __ n t

WORD WISE

If a word in the list is spelled correctly, you can find it in the puzzle. Circle each word that you find and cross it off the list. (Words may appear in any direction.)

If the word is not spelled correctly in the word list, it is not in the puzzle. Write it correctly in the one of the blanks.

Word List:

E	V	H	D	E	R	U	S	I	E	L	Y	L	T	S	A	H	G
L	C	Y	R	E	T	E	M	E	C	U	J	B	C	P	M	L	Y
I	S	S	Y	G	L	B	A	P	Y	T	Y	O	K	S	I	S	U
N	N	U	Y	A	J	I	O	F	D	L	R	K	K	J	Y	T	I
E	V	V	O	L	M	T	V	M	T	R	I	R	Y	E	A	N	R
V	T	E	V	I	P	M	A	E	E	L	C	E	T	K	J	E	R
U	T	R	X	O	C	R	E	S	R	H	K	S	N	T	M	M	E
J	Y	E	U	H	R	S	P	L	A	Y	U	R	E	U	I	N	L
I	Y	R	N	I	I	O	N	N	I	O	L	L	M	L	M	O	E
S	R	E	A	E	N	L	D	O	I	D	H	O	E	W	A	R	V
I	U	G	C	D	I	E	A	C	C	P	T	A	V	R	N	I	A
U	E	O	E	N	L	G	I	R	M	N	G	U	L	E	E	V	N
E	L	N	L	I	A	P	Y	A	A	E	U	F	O	S	U	N	T
P	C	M	E	O	S	V	P	H	Y	T	A	V	V	T	V	E	B
E	I	R	U	U	V	P	E	S	X	U	I	J	N	L	E	R	O
L	T	N	S	V	G	I	C	I	C	B	U	O	I	I	R	N	W
E	S	S	A	P	M	I	R	E	R	J	J	S	N	N	D	Y	X
U	E	P	D	S	N	R	T	F	B	G	N	R	T	G	R	D	J

CEMETERY
CHANDELIER
CONGRADULATIONS
CORRESPONDENCE
DELIVERY
DETERENT
DILEMMA
ENVIRONMENT
EXHILARATION
FAUCET
FLOURESCENT
FRIVOLOUS
GHASTLY
GRIEVANCE
HYGIENE
IMPASSE
INVOLVEMENT
IRRELEVANT
JUVENILE
LEISURE
MANAGMENT
MANEUVER
MARRIAGE
MAYONAISE
MILEAGE
NUETRAL
OCASSION
PAMPHLET
POTPOURRI
PRIVILEDGE
STUDIOES
SUSPICIOUS
UNCONSCIOUS
VENGENCE
WRESTLING

_____ _____

_____ _____

_____ _____

_____ _____

©Ann Richmond Fisher
The Spelling Bee Toolbox for Grades 6-8

TRANSPORTATION TROUBLES

How did the stranded writer finally get across the ocean? Use the clues to unscramble each word. Then write your answers in the diagram.

1. having doubts: c l a t e s i k p
2. very serious: m o s e n l
3. threatening harm: s m o o n i u
4. perplexing situation: m i l d e a m
5. evil character: l i n i v a l
6. spooky spirit: t h o p m a n
7. annoying thing: c a n n i s e u
8. to receive as an heir: r e i n t h i
9. to bring back: v e r r i t e e
10. mixture of objects: r o o t p p u i r

Write the letters from the shaded squares in order in the blanks below to find the answer to the riddle.

How did the writer get across the ocean?

He took the _ _ _ _ _ _ _ _ _ _ _ _ !

On the back of this page, write a sentence for each of the ten words above.

©Ann Richmond Fisher
The Spelling Bee Toolbox for Grades 6-8

AMPLE ADJECTIVES

How many adjectives do you know that are spelled with exactly ten letters? Here is a list of 15, but the words have been split into letter pairs and then scrambled.

voluminous, commodious,..

To spell each adjective, choose one letter pair from the first column, one from the second column, and so on. Write the completed word in the blank beside the first two letters. An example is shown.

ARTIFICIAL	1. AR	~~ST~~	IG	YA	NT
_____	2. BE	AM	LL	VA	ED
_____	3. DI	BS	ST	IB	NT
_____	4. FL	NE	EM	AB	~~AL~~
_____	5. IR	CY	PO	RO	NT
_____	6. VA	~~TI~~	EQ	AT	LE
_____	7. ME	RE	CU	AB	US
_____	8. NE	NI	VO	IF	NT
_____	9. SY	RI	CE	AT	LE
_____	10. OM	TI	LE	~~CI~~	NT
_____	11. NO	GL	EG	LO	LE
_____	12. SC	SA	NT	LE	IC
_____	13. SU	FA	CL	IB	US
_____	14. RE	TI	~~FI~~	UE	LE
_____	15. IN	IE	BO	TE	IC

Write sentences using ten of these adjectives on the back of this page.

Mnemonic Tricks

A mnemonic (ni-mon-ik) device is something that helps you remember an important fact.

If only I could remember how to spell mnemonic!

1. List 8 words that are difficult to remember how to spell.

2. Write a mnemonic phrase or sentence for each one in the chart below. For example, to help you remember the correct spelling of FRIEND, you might write *Fred Runs In Everyone's Neighborhood Daily*.

3. On the back of this page, draw a picture to go with at least two of your mnemonic tricks. For the example of FRIEND, you could draw a sketch of man running down a neighborhood street.

Spelling Word	Mnemonic Trick(s)
friend	*Fred Runs In Everyone's Neighborhood Daily*
1.	
2.	
3.	
4.	
5.	
6.	
7.	
8.	

from **AnyWord™ Partner Activities,** © 2012 Ann Richmond Fisher
www.spelling-words-well.com/anyword-spelling-worksheets-ebooks.html

ANSWERS TO WORKSHEETS

Tough Choice

1. spacious
2. preferable
3. fierce
4. contagious
5. foreign
6. sincerely
7. familiar
8. unmistakable
9. disastrous
10. recyclable
11. contagious
12. fierce

Fit for Four

1. negotiate
2. surveillance
3. technically
4. undoubtedly
5. variegated
6. propeller
7. ordinarily
8. sophomore
9. phenomenon
10. parallel
11. vegetable
12. potential
13. tomatoes
14. vaccinate
15. retrieve
16. separately
17. newsstand
18. obedient
19. numerator
20. turbulent

Word Wise

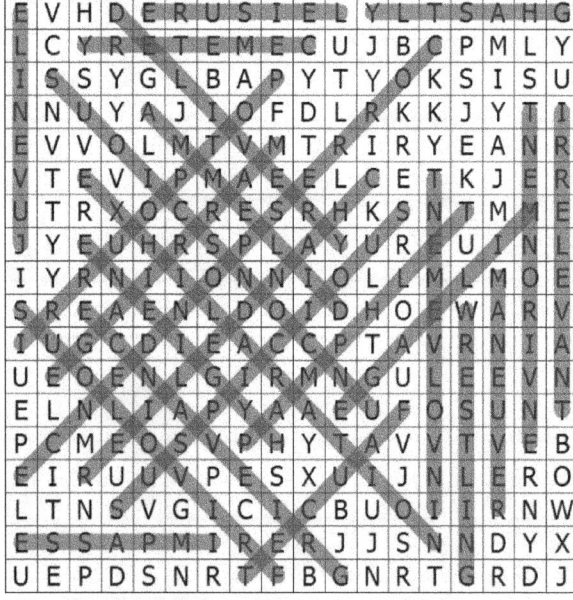

Misspelled words spelled correctly:

congratulations   neutral
deterrent   occasion
fluorescent   privilege
management   studios
mayonnaise   vengeance

Order, Please

1. ability
2. abstain
3. accelerate
4. accept
5. accessible
6. accidentally
7. accommodate
8. achievement
9. acquaintance
10. acquittal
11. aerial
12. ambassador
13. amnesty
14. analysis
15. ancestor
16. ancient
17. apostrophe
18. apparatus
19. appearance
20. appreciate

1. appreciate
2. appearance
3. apparatus
4. apostrophe
5. ancient
6. ancestor
7. analysis
8. amnesty
9. ambassador
10. aerial
11. acquittal
12. acquaintance
13. achievement
14. accommodate
15. accidentally
16. accessible
17. accept
18. accelerate
19. abstain
20. ability

Transportation Troubles

S	K	E	P	T	I	C	A	L
S	O	L	E	M	N			
O	M	I	N	O	U	S		
D	I	L	E	M	M	A		
V	I	L	L	A	I	N		
P	H	A	N	T	O	M		
N	U	I	S	A	N	C	E	
	I	N	H	E	R	I	T	
R	E	T	R	I	E	V	E	
P	O	T	P	O	U	R	R	I

Ample Adjectives

2. benevolent
3. disastrous
4. flamboyant
5. irrelevant
6. variegated
7. meticulous
8. negligible
9. systematic
10. omnipotent
11. noticeable
12. scientific
13. subsequent
14. recyclable
15. infallible

©Ann Richmond Fisher
The Spelling Bee Toolbox for Grades 6-8

THE SPELLING BEE TOOLBOX ™
Frequently Asked Questions

Question: Why are there easy words at the beginning of the big list of words and sentences in the Toolbox?

Answer: There are easy words so that *all* of your students may enjoy participating in a spelling bee! The Toolbox is designed for general school and community use, with the idea that as many students as possible will want to be included. Many times, most students can succeed through at least the first round and feel successful.

As explained in the directions, please feel free to skip over any words that way too easy, or otherwise unsuitable for your purposes. I've included a huge list of words so you should still have plenty!

Question: Should students be given the entire list of words to study before the bee?

Answer: This depends on your philosophy and preference. Some educators feel that it is most fair when all students are given the exact words to study in advance. It "levels the playing field."

Others believe that this method only rewards those who can memorize the best, rather than those who can actually spell the best. By not giving students the entire list, the bee will reward students who can think on their feet, who have large spelling vocabularies, and who have studied on their own.

My recommendation is to use the 100-word study list provided in the Toolbox. About 70 of these words are in the actual big list. This gives students a taste of what to expect in the bee. Encourage students to study difficult words on their own, as well as to follow other tips included in this eBook.

Question: When conducting the spelling bee, should I use the words in the order they appear in the list of words and sentences, or mix them up randomly?

Answer: I strongly encourage you to use them in the order the appear. That's because the words are, generally speaking, arranged from easiest to most difficult. It makes sense to have the easiest words at the beginning of the bee. As spellers are eliminated, the remaining spellers should be given tougher and tougher words.

For example, it wouldn't be good for a speller to given *boulevard* in the first round, misspell it and be eliminated, then for another speller to be given the word *under* in the sixth round and advance. (Please note that you may want to rearrange a few words a bit since difficulty is always somewhat subjective and can vary by curriculum, etc.)

If you are giving students all the words to study in advance, use the alphabetical list of words, rather than the list of words and sentences.

©Ann Richmond Fisher

www. spelling-words-well.com

The Spelling Bee Toolbox for Grades 6-8

THE SPELLING BEE TOOLBOX™
Spelling Bee Words and Sentences

See instructions on page 7. To see all the words included in the list, please refer to the alphabetical listing on page 69.

1. grasp – She tried to grasp the rope and climb back up the mountain.

2. future – In the future, Mike plans to live in France.

3. copies – Please make ten copies of this document.

4. junior – Ben is a junior in high school.

5. climate – Some people feel better when they live in a warm climate.

6. mammal – A cow is a mammal.

7. jealous – Susan was jealous of Tracy's new shoes.

8. energy – A two-year-old child has a lot of energy.

9. circle – Circle the correct answers with your pencil.

10. regular – My dad drinks regular coffee.

11. pattern – Find the next number in this pattern.

12. whoever – Whoever left the window open should close it.

13. roam – My little sister likes to roam around the backyard.

14. service – We received excellent service at this restaurant.

15. accept – Please accept this birthday gift.

16. hunger – Thousands of people die from hunger every day.

17. fraction – One-half is a common fraction.

18. island – We must take a boat to reach the island.

19. pledge – Everyone said a pledge to the flag before the program began.

20. passenger – I was the last passenger to get off the bus.

21. yield – Cars should always yield to pedestrians.

22. factory – The new factory will make furniture.

23. blown – The wind has blown hard every night this week.

24. solar – We put solar panels on the roof of our house.

25. sketch – He drew a quick sketch of his dog.

26. furrow – Grandad will always furrow his eyebrows when he's deep in thought.

27. journey – It was a long journey on foot through the desert.

28. canyon – It was impossible to cross the deep canyon.

29. luggage – Mary took three pieces of luggage on the plane.

30. museum – The history museum has a display of Egyptian artifacts.

31. studios – Artists often have large windows in their studios.

32. southern – The southern breeze brought warmth to the land.

33. tunnel – The cell phone call was dropped when we drove through the tunnel.

34. wives – The wives went shopping while the husbands played golf.

35. treasure – The pirates buried their treasure under a palm tree.

36. surface – When water boils, bubbles form on the surface.

37. audience – The audience cheered wildly at the concert.

38. myth - An urban myth is often a popular, but untrue.

39. sentence – Every sentence has a subject and a predicate.

40. thoughtful – Emily gives very thoughtful gifts to her friends.

41. channel – You can use the remote to change the channel.

42. marriage – The marriage vows are an important part of the wedding ceremony.

43. argued – The lawyers argued their case in court.

44. diaries – People often lock their diaries so others cannot read them.

45. choir – The school choir gave a Christmas concert.

46. thicken – Bob likes to thicken the gravy before he serves it.

47. threat – There's a threat of a serious snowstorm tonight.

48. minute – If you can wait one more minute, I will help you with your project.

49. salute – The soldier will salute his commander.

50. reptile – The reptile exhibit included snakes and alligators.

51. depth – At some points, the depth of the Pacific Ocean is over 10,000 meters.

52. exercise – Daily exercise is good for the body and the brain.

53. beliefs – His religious beliefs influence the way he lives.

54. cleanse – It's important to thoroughly cleanse a wound to prevent infection.

55. loaves – Grandma brought us three loaves of homemade bread.

56. caution – Proceed with caution through a dangerous intersection.

57. piano – Keith started playing the piano when he was seven.

58. attract – Wearing perfume will often attract insects.

59. ratio – The ratio of apples to oranges in this basket is two to one.

60. capable – I am perfectly capable of walking to the post office by myself.

61. digestion – Mom says that drinking lots of water is good for your digestion.

62. electricity – We lost electricity when a tree fell on the lines outside our house.

63. invisible – The wind is invisible but its effects are not.

64. spaghetti – Spaghetti is one of my favorite foods.

65. telephones – All of the network's telephones stopped working at the same time.

66. equator – Temperatures are warmest closest to the equator.

67. pollution – Water pollution killed some of the fish in the river.

68. principal – The principal visited our classroom yesterday.

69. variety – It's best to eat a variety of fresh fruits and vegetables.

70. manor – The manor was surrounded by a high stone wall.

71. faucet – Because the faucet leaked, it had to be replaced.

72. avoid – If you are diabetic, you should avoid eating foods with a lot of sugar.

73. fireproof – The safe for important documents was made of fireproof materials.

74. echoes – We heard echoes from the wolves coming across the valley.

75. importance – The matter was of great importance to everyone in the room.

76. grief – Tina was filled with grief at the passing of her cat.

77. envelope – Remember to put a stamp on the envelope.

78. official – The government official did not want to comment on the matter.

79. safety – For your safety, please keep your hands inside the car at all times.

80. mute – Because the phone was on mute, my friend could not hear me.

81. creature – Big Foot was a mythical creature.

82. calendar – At the beginning of each month, I always tear a page off the calendar.

83. delivery – Joe has a delivery job for a florist.

84. requirement – It is a requirement that Tom wear a uniform on his job.

85. arithmetic – Addition and subtraction are important parts of arithmetic.

86. ancient – The ancient Greeks held the first Olympic games.

87. vantage – From my vantage point, it seems wisest to leave on vacation at once.

88. governor – The governor is the highest elected official in our state.

89. mourn – Many people gathered to mourn the loss of their friend.

90. demonstrate – I asked the salesman to demonstrate the phone's new features.

91. exterior – We bought exterior paint to use on the outside of our house.

92. hyphen – Use a hyphen when writing numbers like *twenty-one*.

93. numerator – The numerator is the top number in a fraction.

94. routine – The dance routine was difficult to learn.

95. crisis – The long drought created a severe crisis for large numbers of people.

96. rhythmic – The rhythmic section of the band is fun to watch.

97. scissors – Children's scissors are rounded on the ends.

98. percent – Ten percent of students in my school are absent on any single day.

99. remarkable – It is remarkable how quickly my baby sister is learning to walk!

100. sword – An antique sword was sold to a collector of old weapons.

101. encouragement – Your cheerful words were a great source of encouragement.

102. cushion – Some people like to sit on the floor on a cushion.

103. chiefs – The police chiefs from ten cities met to discuss public safety.

104. frontal – The commander ordered a frontal attack on the enemy's camp.

105. novel – Many people would like to write a novel.

106. curious – Many cats are known for being curious.

107. sponge – Meg used a sponge to wipe up the spilled water.

108. rural – There are many farms in rural areas.

109. zealous – Rioters were zealous to oust the dictator who had illegally seized power.

110. physical – You must have an annual physical exam to be on a sports team.

111. alternative – We hated to cancel the trip, but the blizzard left us no alternative.

112. personal – The Prime Minister is a close personal friend.

113. cupboard – There's plenty of soup in the cupboard.

114. replacement – The band members need to find a replacement for their lead singer.

115. autumn – Autumn is my favorite time of year.

116. senior – The senior executive was also the owner of the company.

117. satisfy – I hope this stew will satisfy your hunger.

118. coupon – With a coupon, this gallon of milk cost less than a dollar.

119. misunderstand – It's easy to misunderstand someone on a bad phone connection.

120. ability – Her ability to get along with people was the reason she always had a job.

121. wrinkle – My best slacks always wrinkle when I sit down.

122. shampoo – The newest shampoo smells like plums.

123. trophies – She keeps all of her sports trophies on the mantle.

124. damaged – The damaged canned goods were sold at a lower price.

125. cease – When the tornado siren sounds, please cease all work and take cover.

126. muscle – She uses an electric massager to relieve the tight muscle in her neck.

127. plumber – We called the plumber when the pipes in the basement burst.

128. tutor – Tim goes to a tutor to learn Arabic.

129. vein – The nurse drew blood from the vein in the patient's arm.

130. comfortable – A recliner is a comfortable chair.

131. dangerous – A dangerous shark swam near the shore.

132. underneath – I found my homework underneath my pillow.

133. approach – We need to learn the best way to approach this difficult problem.

134. penalties – The hockey team had no penalties during the first period of the game.

135. toxin – Scientists are working to identify the toxin that killed all the fish in the lake.

136. wrestling – Fourteen wrestlers competed in the wrestling tournament.

137. ambulance – All the cars pulled off the road when the ambulance came by.

138. average – My grades have always been above average.

139. contribute – Every year we contribute to the Humane Society.

140. interview – The President said he would give a five-minute interview.

141. galaxy – Our galaxy is just one of many in the universe.

142. fierce – Many wild animals are especially fierce when hungry.

143. knitting – Grandma has been knitting since she was ten years old.

144. garbled – The telemarketer's voice sounded garbled on the phone.

145. vegetable – My favorite vegetable is corn.

146. violence – We decided not to watch the movie because it had so much violence.

147. unbelievable – We have received an unbelievable amount of rain this summer!

148. systematic – The detective took a systematic approach to searching the grounds.

149. mechanic – Our mechanic is able to repair any kind of car.

150. noticeable – Her new hair color was very noticeable.

151. struggling – I've been struggling all day to solve this brain teaser.

152. unsuccessful – My attempts to phone my senator have been unsuccessful.

153. preferable – It's preferable to come to school late than to not come at all.

154. appearance – The rock star made a guest appearance on a TV show.

155. unmistakable – A skunk gives off an unmistakable odor.

156. emergency – Three emergency vehicles raced through the intersection.

157. elevator – We took the elevator to the tenth floor.

158. excellent – Many animals have excellent hearing.

159. recyclable – Newspaper is a recyclable material.

160. nationality – The nationality of each immigrant was represented by a flag.

161. applaud – Everyone wanted to applaud the speech.

162. dessert – Dessert is sometimes the best part of the meal!

163. forehead – I have a sunburn on my forehead because I forgot to wear a hat.

164. extremely – Kelsie was extremely tired after the three-hour swim practice.

165. diamond – The diamond fell out of Mom's wedding ring.

166. beige – We used beige paint on the walls.

167. budget – Going out for dinner tonight is not in our weekly budget.

168. equipment – Computer equipment quickly becomes outdated.

169. inventory – The store closed for one day so the employees could take inventory.

170. departure – The plane's departure was delayed by fog.

171. radius – The diameter of a circle is twice as long as its radius.

172. disastrous – Drinking while driving often leads to disastrous results.

173. musical – It took weeks to learn all the songs for the musical.

174. accidentally – I accidentally deleted an important file on the computer.

175. experience – My trip to China was a once-in-a-lifetime experience.

176. coarse – Sam used coarse sandpaper to smooth the wooden table.

177. familiar – The road back to his hometown looked very familiar.

178. neighborhood – Our neighborhood has a big yard sale every summer.

179. embargo – An embargo was imposed on grain from the foreign country.

180. statues – These statues will be moved to another museum.

181. hangar – My uncle stores his airplane in a hangar.

182. occasion – A high school graduation is a very special occasion.

183. raisin – A raisin is a dried grape.

184. foreign – Foreign diplomats have special privileges.

185. coyote – The coyote howled at the moon.

186. referred – Dan referred to the owner's manual when the device quit working.

187. bough – The bough hung so low on the tree that it was easy to climb.

188. headache – The bright lights gave her a bad headache.

189. habitat – The habitat of the rain forest is not suitable for polar bears.

190. endurance – A runner must have endurance to finish a marathon.

191. controlled – Amy's allergies were controlled well with a new medication.

192. heritage – A love for nature is part of my heritage.

193. cooperation – We will need everyone's cooperation to finish the task on time.

194. ingredient – No one knows the secret ingredient in Martha's cake.

195. distributed – The political candidate distributed thousands of flyers.

196. dyed – The bridesmaids dyed their shoes to match the color of their dresses.

197. nurture – It's natural to want to nurture a newborn baby.

198. valuable – Please place your valuable items in the hotel safe.

199. diameter – The diameter of a penny is about two centimeters.

200. logical – The logical result of spending more money than you make is bankruptcy.

201. examination – He made a close examination of the coins before buying them.

202. omitted – The news story omitted the location of the event.

203. comply – You'll have to comply with our policies if you want to work here.

204. oasis – Desert travelers were relieved to see an oasis on the horizon.

205. category – Select one item under each category.

206. ordinarily – Ordinarily, he makes no exceptions on his homework policy.

207. controversial – His controversial views on taxes probably cost him the election.

208. popularity – The popularity of teen pop star only grew as he got older.

209. fiasco – The curtain tore as the play opened, and the rest of the night was a fiasco.

210. fossilize – Many plants will fossilize over time.

211. cemetery – The funeral was followed by a short service at the cemetery.

212. emphasize – I want to emphasize the importance of following the directions.

213. abandon – Sometimes people abandon their unwanted pets.

214. mileage – He calculated the mileage for each sales call.

215. tongue – The little girls stuck out her tongue at the mean cashier.

216. puny – The runt of the litter was indeed puny.

217. sincerely – I sincerely hope we can finish this puzzle tonight.

218. rustic – The family loved their vacation in the rustic log cabin.

219. newsstand – Dad buys his newspaper at a newsstand every morning.

220. putter – On Saturday mornings, we like to putter around the house.

221. faulty – The fire was caused by faulty electrical wiring.

222. bouquet – Jim surprised his wife with a bouquet of roses.

223. advise – Ask an expert to advise you before investing in gold.

224. phantom – The criminal was haunted by phantoms of his victims.

225. jewelry – The woman's gold jewelry was worth a fortune.

226. contagious – Colds are contagious, so please cover your mouth when you sneeze.

227. separately – The guests all arrived at the party separately.

228. leisure – In her leisure time, she likes to read and play golf.

229. spacious – She enjoyed her spacious new home after living in a tiny apartment.

230. biscuit – He likes to put honey on his biscuit.

231. influence – I won't try to influence you if you've already made up your mind.

232. havoc – The energetic puppy wreaked havoc in the tidy office.

233. cinnamon – Cinnamon tastes good in applesauce.

234. interruption – She welcomed the interruption of a phone call from an old friend.

235. illegal – Selling cigarettes to minors is illegal.

236. campaign – The campaign for President often lasts for years.

237. congratulations – We offered our congratulations to the newlyweds.

238. bizarre – In a bizarre turn of events, two police cars collided.

239. bagel – I like to put cream cheese on my bagel.

240. celery – Celery and carrots make a healthy snack.

241. voucher – Use this voucher to get a free pizza.

242. saga – We now rejoin the on-going saga of Kim, Mark and their lost puppy.

243. frugal – Because Esther is frugal, she reuses sandwich bags and bread wrappers.

244. roommate – My college roommate became a very good friend.

245. frantic – One hour before the wedding, the bride's mother was extremely frantic.

246. consequence – Most actions have a natural consequence.

247. statistics – Sports fans generally learn a lot of statistics about their favorite teams.

248. bureau – She placed her clothes inside the drawers of the old bureau.

249. achievement – The student was recognized for outstanding achievement.

250. impossibility – Walking up stairs wearing stilts, for most people, is an impossibility.

251. coincide – My birthday will coincide with Thanksgiving this year.

252. analysis – After doing a thorough analysis, the buyer chose the best house.

253. ghetto – Poverty is rampant in the ghetto.

254. economics – Betsy studies economics because she enjoys analysis and numbers.

255. dismissal – There will be early dismissal from school because of bad weather.

256. environment – Cleaning up litter is good for the environment.

257. meteor – We believe a meteor landed here many years ago.

258. executive – The executive took a cut in pay because of company losses.

259. cringe – I cringe when I hear my friend scrape her fingernails on a chalkboard.

260. democracy – In a democracy, people should take advantage of the right to vote.

261. negotiate – The owners tried to negotiate a fair settlement with their employees.

262. penicillin – Penicillin is an important medicine for combating some infections.

263. hostile – It's hard to enjoy your job if you feel you're in an hostile environment.

264. individual – Cheese sticks are sold in individual packets.

265. shear – The farmer will shear his sheep in the spring.

266. immobilize – I have to immobilize my broken arm for six weeks.

267. heroic – In an heroic act, the fireman went into a burning house to save the child.

268. idle – It's hard to watch someone who is idle when there's so much work to do!

269. irresistible – I fought an irresistible urge to sneeze all during the prayer.

270. violation – The speeding violation cost her $200.

271. irate – The man was irate when he learned someone had stolen his credit card.

272. academic – First year law students carry a heavy academic load.

273. fulfill – He will fulfill the last requirement for the job when he passes the math test.

274. advantageous – It would be advantageous for you to start a savings account now.

275. souvenir – I purchased a souvenir mug from every city I visited.

276. acquaintance – The mayor is an acquaintance of mine.

277. sophomore – In tenth grade, you'll be known as a sophomore.

278. laboratory – Inside the laboratory, conditions must be sterile.

279. athlete – The top athlete in each sport was awarded a trophy.

280. culprit – The teacher wanted to find the culprit who put glue on her chair.

281. liquidation – The appliance store had very low prices during its liquidation sale.

282. hygiene – It's difficult for the homeless to maintain good personal hygiene.

283. grievance - The man filed a grievance when he was fired from his job.

284. graffiti – Some graffiti could be considered art; some merely defaces property.

285. gossiping – The two women were always gossiping about their boss.

286. suspicious – A man lurking outside the door looked very suspicious.

287. changeable – Weather in Michigan can be very changeable.

288. legibly – Please write your name legibly on this document.

289. scarcity – In some regions of the world, there is a scarcity of life-saving medicines.

290. harass – If you continue to harass me, I will have to report you.

291. skeptical – Mom is always skeptical of door-to-door sales people.

292. simile – *I'm as hungry as a horse* is an example of a simile.

293. maneuver – It can be hard to maneuver a large truck into a small parking space.

294. recipe – The recipe calls for six cups of flour.

295. murmur – Every time he tried to speak, a murmur went through the crowd.

296. artificial – It's hard to tell that the tree is artificial.

297. justifiable – The jury felt the man's actions were justifiable in his situation.

298. perspective – To understand our perspective, you should live in our community for a few years.

299. pedestrian – The pedestrian was struck by a car that ran through a stoplight.

300. pageant – The winner of the pageant will win a college scholarship.

301. traitor – The traitor was despised by those he betrayed.

302. amnesty – Granting amnesty to illegal immigrants is a controversial topic.

303. visualize – If I can visualize the city map, I'll know how to get to the right address.

304. transferring – Tomorrow I'll be transferring my money to a new bank.

305. fatigue – Because of chronic fatigue, Sue takes a long nap every day.

306. vigorously – Shake the juice vigorously before drinking.

307. conductor – The symphony rehearsed with a guest conductor.

308. forgery – At once, the bank teller knew the check was a forgery.

309. ancestor – Every ancestor on his family tree came from Ireland.

310. occasionally – Occasionally, I like to get up early on Saturdays to read a book.

311. recruit – The coach wanted to recruit the best players for his team.

312. gauge – You can't always gauge your success by the amount of money you make.

313. exhausted – After babysitting five young children, Lisa came home exhausted.

314. secretary – When the secretary was ill, the phone went unanswered.

315. juvenile – That wallpaper looks too juvenile to in put a teenager's bedroom.

316. attendance – He was given special recognition for perfect attendance.

317. negligent – Because the doctor was negligent, the patient needed further surgery.

318. confetti – The concert ended with a flurry of confetti.

319. qualifying – You must make a qualifying purchase to receive the free gift card.

320. desolate – The land was desolate because of the prolonged drought.

321. lunar – The lunar eclipse was spectacular.

322. parachute – The parachute opened right on time, allowing him to land gently.

323. venom – The venom from some snakes is poisonous.

324. fascinating – I read a fascinating biography about an early explorer.

325. scholar – The visiting scholar studied literature.

326. genuine – He searched for a genuine fossil along the beach.

327. marvelous – We had a marvelous day at the beach.

328. overwhelming – Planning the party for 600 guests was indeed overwhelming.

329. exhilaration – John felt a sense of exhilaration as he parachuted for the first time.

330. approximately – Dinner will be ready in approximately one hour.

331. infamous – The city is infamous for its high rate of poverty and crime.

332. abbreviation – Use the abbreviation for your country when completing the form.

333. inspiration – The injured veteran was an inspiration to all who met him.

334. scenery – The scenery for the play was painted on plywood.

335. parallel – Two parallel lines will never intersect.

336. bankruptcy – The company filed for bankruptcy because it could not pay its bills.

337. management – This store is now under new management.

338. chaperone – Teachers usually chaperone the school dances.

339. extraordinary – The young child's musical ability is quite extraordinary.

340. encircle – Fans encircle the superstar wherever she goes.

341. solemn – Everyone was very solemn as the will was being read.

342. involvement – Her involvement in the charity event was greatly appreciated.

343. imaginary – Many kids have imaginary friends.

344. vanquish – Ned was able to vanquish all his fears and finally go skydiving.

345. guarantee – The phone came with a one-year guarantee against defects.

346. absorb – Some paper towels can absorb a lot of water.

347. opinion – The news article was really more of an opinion piece.

348. canine – Only specially trained officers work in the canine unit.

349. impartial – A judge must be impartial when presiding over a trial.

350. appreciate – To truly appreciate food, sometimes you must go hungry.

351. inherit – Judy will one day inherit her mother's jewelry.

352. definitely – The second peanut butter definitely tastes better than the first one.

353. binoculars – Use the binoculars to get a closer look at the exotic bird.

354. specific – We want to improve, but we lack a plan with specific details.

355. awesome – The sunset on the beach was an awesome sight.

356. tremor – Another tremor was felt several days after the earthquake.

357. obedient – Teaching a dog to be obedient requires much perseverance.

358. relieve – She took an aspirin to relieve the pain in her knee.

359. endeavor – Trying to land a person on the moon was a daunting endeavor.

360. burglary – The burglary went unreported because the victim was away.

361. accessible – The concert hall is accessible by wheelchair.

362. aerial – From the helicopter, the aerial view of the mountain is breath-taking.

363. gorgeous – Many thought the 80-year-old actress was still gorgeous.

364. counsel – The minister wanted to counsel the couple before their wedding.

365. diagnosis – He welcomed the cancer-free diagnosis.

366. anxious – The anxious mother kept checking her phone messages.

367. crypt – Many deceased members of the society were buried in the crypt.

368. gymnasium – A new floor was installed in the gymnasium before the big game.

369. persuade – Jack always tries to persuade me that he's right.

370. fashionable – Large women's hats are quite fashionable in some places.

371. messenger – The messenger waited to deliver a reply.

372. applicant – Each job applicant was required to undergo a background test.

373. stationery – Let's use the business stationery when we write a letter to the mayor.

374. adolescent – The adolescent no longer enjoyed playing with his little brother.

375. uncontrollable – She had an uncontrollable urge to eat chocolate ice cream.

376. lieutenant – The lieutenant ordered his men into battle.

377. miniature – Helen collects miniature spoons.

378. pamphlet – The pamphlet was printed in full color.

379. chandelier – The beautiful chandelier was made of lead crystal.

380. vacuum – Because our dog sheds a lot, we have to vacuum the rugs everyday.

381. withhold – The government will withhold taxes from my paycheck.

382. oases – There is often a great distance between two oases in a desert.

383. nuisance – This broken finger is a real nuisance when I'm on a keyboard.

384. dialogue – The dialogue was hard to follow because the actors mumbled.

385. asphalt – The smell of asphalt from the new parking lot crept into the building.

386. architect – The architect designed an unusual a new office complex.

387. colleague – My colleague and I will be making a presentation next week.

388. politician – A politician decided to run for reelection.

389. unique – Toby's singing voice has a very unique quality.

390. sieve – Pour the canned peas through a sieve to get rid of the extra liquid.

391. hazardous – Hazardous materials must be handled in the proper fashion.

392. awkward – She felt awkward the first time she tried to do a somersault.

393. accumulate – The vagabond tried not to accumulate many possessions.

394. mayonnaise – Mayonnaise tastes good on chicken sandwiches.

395. neutral – The referees in any game should remain neutral.

396. acknowledgement – The writer received an acknowledgement for her work.

397. acquittal – The wrongly-convicted man finally received an acquittal.

398. amateur – Amateur athletes, while not paid, still have a lot of fun.

399. apostrophe – Remember to insert the apostrophe when writing a contraction.

400. chameleon – It was hard to spot the chameleon in the sand.

401. archeology – Because she loves history, she decided to major in archeology.

402. asthma – She could not participate in the race because she has asthma.

403. solidarity – Acting in solidarity, all the workers agreed to donate a day's wages to a needy coworker.

404. percolator – Dad prefers coffee that is brewed in a percolator.

405. colonel – The colonel wondered if he would ever become a general.

406. critique – Her critique of the movie was quite harsh.

407. deterrent – The fence served as a deterrent against trespassers.

408. discrepancy – There was a discrepancy between the posted price and my receipt.

409. equilibrium – It's easy to lose your equilibrium if you have fluid in your ears.

410. escalator – Because the escalator was not working, we had to use the stairs.

411. occurring – To prevent burns from occurring, always use oven mitts when cooking.

412. extricate - Emergency personnel had to extricate the injured woman from her car.

413. flamboyant – The flamboyant actress wears red furs and purple sequins.

414. frivolous – Don't get side-tracked by frivolous talk in the middle of a crisis.

415. necessity – Water is a basic necessity for life.

416. obstinate – The child remained obstinate even when his father punished him.

417. outrageous – The price of gasoline is outrageous!

418. grotesque – The monster mask was particularly grotesque in the dim moonlight.

419. haphazard - Working in a haphazard manner, the man nailed his jeans to the wall.

420. insufficient – The evidence was insufficient to convict the accused man.

421. rehearsal – The night before the show opened, rehearsal lasted for three hours.

422. obsolete – The floppy disk for storing computer data is now obsolete.

423. interrogate – The police will interrogate the suspect at the police station.

424. propeller – The airplane's propeller was damaged in the crash.

425. luncheon – The luncheon was in honor of Mother's Day.

426. malicious – A malicious virus threatened to destroy thousands of hard drives.

427. innumerable – We swatted innumerable flies inside the house.

428. plaintiff – The plaintiff filed a complaint against a popular businessman.

429. nostalgia – She looked through the family photo album with smiles of nostalgia.

430. serviceable – This car is old, but it should be serviceable for several more years.

431. mischievous – Ben had a mischievous look in his eye as he walked away.

432. unenforceable – The anti-texting traffic law was good, but unenforceable.

433. prosperous – While many thought he was prosperous, he was, in fact, a pauper.

434. precipice – We stood at the precipice of the mountain, too scared to look down.

435. perseverance – It takes perseverance to learn to play an instrument well.

436. catastrophe – The severe earthquake was a natural catastrophe.

437. villain – In the play, the villain wore a black cape.

438. predecessor – The mayor's predecessor left him with a budget shortfall.

439. fallacy – An outdated fallacy is that butter should be put on a burn.

440. technically – The gymnastics routine was technically flawless.

441. unconscious – After the boy fell down the long flight of stairs, he lay unconscious.

442. vivacious – The vivacious cheerleader yelled throughout the entire game.

443. prestigious – The Rhodes and Fulbright scholarships are prestigious awards.

444. malady – She suffers from a malady that her doctors are unable to diagnose.

445. relevant – Please tell the judge only the relevant details of the case.

446. schism – A schism formed in the family over the division of the inheritance.

447. infallible – There is no infallible cure for the common cold.

448. benevolent – The benevolent neighbor gave his needy neighbors a car.

449. vigilant – The vigilant security guard caught the shoplifter.

450. inconvenience – It is an inconvenience for some people to wash their own dishes.

451. envious – Some folks are always envious of others, no matter how much they own.

452. characteristic – He answered the phone with his characteristic growl.

453. honorary – The speaker received an honorary degree from the university.

454. meticulous – She is so meticulous she cleans inside the locks of the doors.

455. contrary – Contrary to what you might think, I do not like your taste in music.

456. privilege – It is a privilege to travel freely throughout this country.

457. deficiency – A vitamin deficiency can cause serious health problems.

458. criminal – The criminal was jailed while awaiting trial.

459. protein – Fish, eggs, meat and cheese all contain high amounts of protein.

460. machinery – Wear safety goggles when operating this machinery.

461. distinctly – I distinctly remember asking you to close the door.

462. feasible – It's not feasible to drive 1,000 miles in one day.

463. correspondence – His correspondence did not mention the time of his arrival.

464. mandatory – Attendance at practice is mandatory if you want to play in the game.

465. quibble – Let's not quibble about such minor points of disagreement.

466. seethe – You could see her seethe in anger when the boss refused to listen.

467. ominous – The ominous clouds meant a heavy snowfall was on its way.

468. abstain – The lawmaker announced she would abstain from the vote.

469. capably – The driver handled the race course very capably.

470. utterance – It seemed that the star's every utterance was made public.

471. profitable – The website proved to be a profitable venture.

472. potential – My teacher always told me I had great potential as a writer.

473. mosquito – The mosquito bite swelled up on her lip.

474. intelligent – The most intelligent reply is often silence.

475. absurd – It's absurd to think that pigs can fly.

476. peril – The ship was in grave peril when the storm arose.

477. retrieve – My dog refuses to retrieve the newspaper.

478. futility – The futility of continuing the picnic in the rain quickly became clear.

479. studious – She's very bright because she's very studious.

480. dormitory – The dormitory closed over the summer break.

481. pronunciation – There is more than one pronunciation for *tomatoes*.

482. frustrate – It's easy to frustrate a child who is just learning to read.

483. skirmish – The skirmish outside the restaurant quickly turned into a big fight.

484. turbulent – Turbulent winds led to the cancellation of the yacht race.

485. phenomenon – Old Faithful is an amazing natural phenomenon.

486. engrossed – He was so engrossed in the novel, he forgot to go to bed.

487. negligible – When the cyclist ran into the bush, the damage was negligible.

488. qualm – At the last minute he had a qualm about purchasing the home.

489. accomplice – My little brother was my accomplice in sneaking the cookies.

490. expensive – The nice restaurant was too expensive for us, so we ate fast food.

491. belligerent – The protestors became more belligerent as the police arrived.

492. cocoon – A beautiful butterfly emerged from the cocoon.

493. authentic – An expert said the signature was authentic.

494. auxiliary – Because of a blackout, the office is running on auxiliary power.

495. chaotic – The three-year-old boy's birthday party quickly became chaotic.

496. pastime – Woodworking is my uncle's favorite pastime.

497. chronic – She received a reprimand for her chronic tardiness.

498. curriculum – The new science curriculum includes more laboratory work.

499. distinction – Ed has the distinction of being the first in his family to go to college.

500. maintenance – A car requires regular maintenance to run properly.

501. drudgery – Pulling weeds in the garden is drudgery to some.

502. scavenger – I felt like a scavenger as I searched every drawer for a nickel.

503. equinox – The first day of spring marks the vernal equinox.

504. swelter – When the air conditioning faltered, people began to swelter.

505. chasm – The earthquake created a chasm too wide to cross.

506. renown (ri-**noun**)– The actor won wide renown for his role in a blockbuster film.

507. surgeon – The surgeon removed the man's appendix.

508. curiosity – His curiosity often put him dangerous predicaments.

509. spontaneous – The pizza party was a completely spontaneous event.

510. etiquette – One rule of etiquette is to say "excuse me" when you burp.

511. facsimile – The document was not an original; it was a facsimile.

512. strenuous – The five-hour climb up the mountain was too strenuous for some.

513. nausea - Some people feel nausea in an airplane.

514. finesse – She makes tiny origami figures with great finesse.

515. handkerchief – Dad pulled out his handkerchief when he sneezed.

516. parliament – The parliament met to vote on a new law.

517. impasse – Negotiations reached an impasse, so a mediator was called in.

518. succinct – The judge appreciated the lawyer's succinct comments.

519. proximity – Wind turbines cannot be in close proximity to airports.

520. espionage – He was suspected of espionage because of his frequent travels.

521. incessant – The incessant noise from the construction site gave me a headache.

522. unforgettable – Winning the tournament was an unforgettable moment for me.

523. indispensable – When Mom is sick, she says I'm an indispensable helper.

524. fictitious – He uses a fictitious name when he writes on others' blogs.

525. labyrinth – The basement corridors formed a confusing labyrinth.

526. playwright – The playwright's dream came true when he saw his work on stage.

527. julienne – The huge salad was topped with julienne strips of ham and cheese.

528. indisputable – There must be indisputable new facts to overturn a ruling.

529. accommodate – The inn can only accommodate ten guests each night.

530. surveillance – Surveillance tapes revealed the perpetrator of the crime.

531. judicious – A judicious decision would be to share the property equally.

532. succumb – If I don't leave a window open, I'll succumb to my overwhelming fatigue and fall asleep at my desk.

533. vaccinate – Doctors like to vaccinate children to protect them from diseases.

534. metamorphosis – A caterpillar undergoes metamorphosis as it becomes a butterfly.

535. notoriety – He gained notoriety when he saved a child from drowning.

536. omnipotent – The words of the religious text honored God for being omnipotent.

537. pandemonium – Pandemonium broke out on the street as the riot began.

538. subterfuge – He resorted to subterfuge to keep his partner from learning the truth.

539. pediatrician – The child's pediatrician prescribed medicine for his cough.

540. irreconcilable – The business partners split up due irreconcilable differences.

541. recipient – Congratulations on being the recipient of a cash award!

542. impropriety –He was accused of impropriety because of the missing funds.

543. tubular – The deep pink flower had a unique tubular bloom.

544. novice – Although I'm a novice kite-flyer, I'm learning quickly to become an expert.

545. dilemma – Every holiday we face the dilemma of which relative to visit first.

546. mortgage – The couple felt great relief when they finally paid off their mortgage.

547. rudimentary – I have only a rudimentary knowledge of algebra, so I won't be able to solve your calculus problem.

548. accompaniment – The accompaniment for her solo was played on the piano.

549. significance – The letter was of such great significance that it was sent overnight.

550. agility – Gymnasts exhibit great agility on the floor exercises.

551. subsequent – Subsequent to getting a new job, he bought a new house.

552. technician – The x-ray technician received her training at a community college.

553. ubiquitous – It seems impossible to kill these ubiquitous little ants!

554. variegated – She knitted the variegated yarn into colorful scarves.

555. undoubtedly – This is undoubtedly the hardest test I've ever taken.

556. versatile – This versatile gadget can slice, dice, mince and chop.

557. scourge – It took decades to overcome the scourge of disease in the impoverished region.

558. picturesque – We enjoyed a picturesque drive through the farmland.

559. synthesis – The synthesis of an unusual melody and erratic rhythm made for some amazing music.

560. vulnerable – Because of waning support, he is vulnerable in the next election.

561. sabotage – We couldn't work because someone sabotaged the assembly line.

562. uncouth – The visitor's behavior was so uncouth that it made us uncomfortable.

563. spasmodic – Some say the Congress has made only spasmodic efforts to reform.

564. grammatically – Each sentence of the report must be grammatically correct.

565. expedient – It's expedient that we leave the island now.

566. ambassador – China's ambassador made a visit to the White House.

567. cavalcade – The cavalcade was made up of 500 soldier on their horses.

568. corroborate – The news reporter could not corroborate the man's story.

569. elimination – He fought for the elimination of age discrimination.

570. hindrance – His backpack was more of a hindrance than a help on the long hike.

571. irrelevant – Your point seems completely irrelevant to our discussion.

572. miscellaneous – She sold lamps, tables and miscellaneous items at the yard sale.

573. melee – A melee broke out when the pirates boarded the ship.

574. accelerate – The driver knew not to accelerate when she hit the patch of ice.

575. amphitheater – The outdoor amphitheater was the site of many summer concerts.

576. callous – Although he sometimes appears callous, the man has a kind heart.

577. colossal – The government spending plan proved to be a colossal failure.

578. derelict – Because she was derelict in her duties, she was fired from her job.

579. facilitate – This outline should facilitate your understanding of the book.

580. inequities – It is not always possible to correct the inequities in life.

581. exemplary – Mrs. Johnson is an exemplary member of our community.

582. forbearance – He handled his many challenges with dignity and forbearance.

583. ghastly – When she realized her error, her face grew ghastly pale.

584. psychologist – The psychologist kept his patient's remarks confidential.

585. hypocritical – It would be hypocritical to ask for donations from others without also making a contribution yourself.

586. incapacitate – The upcoming heart surgery will incapacitate him for several weeks.

587. longevity – My mom's side of the family is known for its longevity.

588. meander – They decided take a long walk and meander through the woods.

589. noncommittal – Despite the enthusiastic sale pitch, the buyer was noncommittal.

590. oscillate – The electric fan was set to oscillate across the room.

591. remembrance – The widow's wedding band was a precious remembrance of her long marriage.

592. pessimism – My friend's constant pessimism makes me gloomy.

593. fluorescent – The fluorescent light bulb flickered for days before it burned out.

594. liaison – The attorney served as a liaison between the birth parents and the adoptive parents.

595. reciprocate – He wanted to reciprocate the kindness I had shown to him.

596. unanimous – The law was passed by an unanimous vote.

597. camouflage – The deer did not see the hunters who were dressed in camouflage.

598. susceptible – Some people are more susceptible to illness than others.

599. recurrent – My account is set up to make recurrent cell phone payments.

600. supersede – The laws of the nation will supersede the laws of the state.

601. misspelled – She gets annoyed when her name is misspelled.

602. rheumatism – Dale moved slowly on cold mornings due to his painful rheumatism.

603. conscientious – A conscientious worker shows up on time and works hard.

604. pseudonym – Mark Twain was a pseudonym used by Samuel Clemens.

605. exaggeration – To say you could eat a horse sounds like an exaggeration to me!

606. apparatus – The breathing apparatus helped him sleep better at night

607. influential – The mayor listens to Sam because he is an influential member of the community.

608. laborious – It's hard to get excited about a long and laborious task.

609. superintendent – The superintendent of schools decides when to cancel school.

610. coercion – The bank teller took money from her drawer under coercion from the armed thief.

611. rapport (ra–**pawr**) – Professor Wyn has excellent rapport with this students.

612. psychiatry – He studied psychiatry because of his interest in the human mind.

613. consciousness – She regained consciousness a few hours after surgery.

614. vengeance – It's not always a good idea to seek vengeance after being wronged.

615. potpourri (**pō**-poo-rē) – The open jar of potpourri released a pleasant fragrance in the room.

616. satisfactorily – He completed the course work satisfactorily and received an A.

617. tableau (ta-**blō**) – The tableau captured the city exactly the way I remembered it.

618. conceivable – Is it conceivable that we could someday live to be 150 years old?

619. acquiesce – In the end, she decided to acquiesce to her parents' curfew.

620. blasphemous – The anti-religious cartoon was seen by many to be blasphemous.

THE SPELLING BEE TOOLBOX™
Alphabetical Listing of Our 620 Spelling Bee Words

1. abandon
2. abbreviation
3. ability
4. absorb
5. abstain
6. absurd
7. academic
8. accelerate
9. accept
10. accessible
11. accidentally
12. accommodate
13. accompaniment
14. accomplice
15. accumulate
16. achievement
17. acknowledgement
18. acquaintance
19. acquiesce
20. acquittal
21. adolescent
22. advantageous
23. advise
24. aerial
25. agility
26. alternative
27. amateur
28. ambassador
29. ambulance
30. amnesty
31. amphitheater
32. analysis
33. ancestor
34. ancient
35. anxious
36. apostrophe
37. apparatus
38. appearance
39. applaud
40. applicant
41. appreciate
42. approach
43. approximately
44. archeology
45. architect
46. argued
47. arithmetic
48. artificial
49. asphalt
50. asthma
51. athlete
52. attendance
53. attract
54. audience
55. authentic
56. autumn
57. auxiliary
58. average
59. avoid
60. awesome
61. awkward
62. bagel
63. bankruptcy
64. beige
65. beliefs
66. belligerent
67. benevolent
68. binoculars
69. biscuit
70. bizarre
71. blasphemous
72. blown
73. bough
74. bouquet
75. budget
76. bureau
77. burglary
78. calendar
79. callous
80. camouflage
81. campaign
82. canine
83. canyon
84. capable
85. capably
86. catastrophe
87. category
88. caution
89. cavalcade
90. cease
91. celery
92. cemetery
93. chameleon
94. chandelier
95. changeable
96. channel
97. chaotic
98. chaperone
99. characteristic
100. chasm
101. chiefs
102. choir
103. chronic
104. cinnamon
105. circle
106. cleanse
107. climate
108. coarse
109. cocoon
110. coercion
111. coincide
112. colleague
113. colonel
114. colossal
115. comfortable
116. comply
117. conceivable
118. conductor
119. confetti
120. congratulations
121. conscientious
122. consciousness
123. consequence

124. contagious
125. contrary
126. contribute
127. controlled
128. controversial
129. cooperation
130. copies
131. correspondence
132. corroborate
133. counsel
134. coupon
135. coyote
136. creature
137. criminal
138. cringe
139. crisis
140. critique
141. crypt
142. culprit
143. cupboard
144. curiosity
145. curious
146. curriculum
147. cushion
148. damaged
149. dangerous
150. deficiency
151. definitely
152. delivery
153. democracy
154. demonstrate
155. departure
156. depth
157. derelict
158. desolate
159. dessert
160. deterrent
161. diagnosis
162. dialogue
163. diameter
164. diamond
165. diaries
166. digestion
167. dilemma
168. disastrous

169. discrepancy
170. dismissal
171. distinction
172. distinctly
173. distributed
174. dormitory
175. drudgery
176. dyed
177. echoes
178. economics
179. electricity
180. elevator
181. elimination
182. embargo
183. emergency
184. emphasize
185. encircle
186. encouragement
187. endeavor
188. endurance
189. energy
190. engrossed
191. envelope
192. envious
193. environment
194. equator
195. equilibrium
196. equinox
197. equipment
198. escalator
199. espionage
200. etiquette
201. exaggeration
202. examination
203. excellent
204. executive
205. exemplary
206. exercise
207. exhausted
208. exhilaration
209. expedient
210. expensive
211. experience
212. exterior
213. extraordinary

214. extremely
215. extricate
216. facilitate
217. facsimile
218. factory
219. fallacy
220. familiar
221. fascinating
222. fashionable
223. fatigue
224. faucet
225. faulty
226. feasible
227. fiasco
228. fictitious
229. fierce
230. finesse
231. fireproof
232. flamboyant
233. fluorescent
234. forbearance
235. forehead
236. foreign
237. forgery
238. fossilize
239. fraction
240. frantic
241. frivolous
242. frontal
243. frugal
244. frustrate
245. fulfill
246. furrow
247. futility
248. future
249. galaxy
250. garbled
251. gauge
252. genuine
253. ghastly
254. ghetto
255. gorgeous
256. gossiping
257. governor
258. graffiti

259. grammatically
260. grasp
261. grief
262. grievance
263. grotesque
264. guarantee
265. gymnasium
266. habitat
267. handkerchief
268. hangar
269. haphazard
270. harass
271. havoc
272. hazardous
273. headache
274. heritage
275. heroic
276. hindrance
277. honorary
278. hostile
279. hunger
280. hygiene
281. hyphen
282. hypocritical
283. idle
284. illegal
285. imaginary
286. immobilize
287. impartial
288. impasse
289. importance
290. impossibility
291. impropriety
292. incapacitate
293. incessant
294. inconvenience
295. indispensable
296. indisputable
297. individual
298. inequities
299. infallible
300. infamous
301. influence
302. influential
303. ingredient
304. inherit
305. innumerable
306. inspiration
307. insufficient
308. intelligent
309. interrogate
310. interruption
311. interview
312. inventory
313. invisible
314. involvement
315. irate
316. irreconcilable
317. irrelevant
318. irresistible
319. island
320. jealous
321. jewelry
322. journey
323. judicious
324. julienne
325. junior
326. justifiable
327. juvenile
328. knitting
329. laboratory
330. laborious
331. labyrinth
332. legibly
333. leisure
334. liaison
335. lieutenant
336. liquidation
337. loaves
338. logical
339. longevity
340. luggage
341. lunar
342. luncheon
343. machinery
344. maintenance
345. malady
346. malicious
347. mammal
348. management
349. mandatory
350. maneuver
351. manor
352. marriage
353. marvelous
354. mayonnaise
355. meander
356. mechanic
357. melee
358. messenger
359. metamorphosis
360. meteor
361. meticulous
362. mileage
363. miniature
364. minute
365. miscellaneous
366. mischievous
367. misspelled
368. misunderstand
369. mortgage
370. mosquito
371. mourn
372. murmur
373. muscle
374. museum
375. musical
376. mute
377. myth
378. nationality
379. nausea
380. necessity
381. negligent
382. negligible
383. negotiate
384. neighborhood
385. neutral
386. newsstand
387. noncommittal
388. nostalgia
389. noticeable
390. notoriety
391. novel
392. novice
393. nuisance

394. numerator
395. nurture
396. oases
397. oasis
398. obedient
399. obsolete
400. obstinate
401. occasion
402. occasionally
403. occurring
404. official
405. ominous
406. omitted
407. omnipotent
408. opinion
409. ordinarily
410. oscillate
411. outrageous
412. overwhelming
413. pageant
414. pamphlet
415. pandemonium
416. parachute
417. parallel
418. parliament
419. passenger
420. pastime
421. pattern
422. pedestrian
423. pediatrician
424. penalties
425. penicillin
426. percent
427. percolator
428. peril
429. perseverance
430. personal
431. perspective
432. persuade
433. pessimism
434. phantom
435. phenomenon
436. physical
437. piano
438. picturesque

439. plaintiff
440. playwright
441. pledge
442. plumber
443. politician
444. pollution
445. popularity
446. potential
447. potpourri
448. precipice
449. predecessor
450. preferable
451. prestigious
452. principal
453. privilege
454. profitable
455. pronunciation
456. propeller
457. prosperous
458. protein
459. proximity
460. pseudonym
461. psychiatry
462. psychologist
463. puny
464. putter
465. qualifying
466. qualm
467. quibble
468. radius
469. raisin
470. rapport
471. ratio
472. recipe
473. recipient
474. reciprocate
475. recruit
476. recurrent
477. recyclable
478. referred
479. regular
480. rehearsal
481. relevant
482. relieve
483. remarkable

484. remembrance
485. renown
486. replacement
487. reptile
488. requirement
489. retrieve
490. rheumatism
491. rhythmic
492. roam
493. roommate
494. routine
495. rudimentary
496. rural
497. rustic
498. sabotage
499. safety
500. saga
501. salute
502. satisfactorily
503. satisfy
504. scarcity
505. scavenger
506. scenery
507. schism
508. scientific
509. scissors
510. scourge
511. secretary
512. seethe
513. senior
514. sentence
515. separately
516. service
517. serviceable
518. shampoo
519. shear
520. sieve
521. significance
522. simile
523. sincerely
524. skeptical
525. sketch
526. skirmish
527. solar
528. solemn

529. solidarity
530. sophomore
531. southern
532. souvenir
533. spacious
534. spaghetti
535. spasmodic
536. specific
537. sponge
538. spontaneous
539. stationery
540. statistics
541. statues
542. strenuous
543. struggling
544. studios
545. studious
546. subsequent
547. subterfuge
548. succinct
549. succumb
550. superintendent
551. supersede
552. surface
553. surgeon
554. surveillance
555. susceptible
556. suspicious
557. swelter
558. sword
559. synthesis
560. systematic
561. tableau
562. technically
563. technician
564. telephones
565. thicken
566. thoughtful
567. threat
568. tongue
569. toxin
570. traitor
571. transferring
572. treasure
573. tremor
574. trophies
575. tubular
576. tunnel
577. turbulent
578. tutor
579. ubiquitous
580. unanimous
581. unbelievable
582. unconscious
583. uncontrollable
584. uncouth
585. underneath
586. undoubtedly
587. unenforceable
588. unforgettable
589. unique
590. unmistakable
591. unsuccessful
592. utterance
593. vaccinate
594. vacuum
595. valuable
596. vanquish
597. vantage
598. variegated
599. variety
600. vegetable
601. vein
602. vengeance
603. venom
604. versatile
605. vigilant
606. vigorously
607. villain
608. violation
609. violence
610. visualize
611. vivacious
612. voucher
613. vulnerable
614. whoever
615. withhold
616. wives
617. wrestling
618. wrinkle
619. yield
620. zealous

THE SPELLING BEE TOOLBOX™
Super Challenge Words

If your spellers manage to breeze through all the words in our list above, use these 20 super-challenge words for your spelling bee. We've included the language of origin, **primary** pronunciation, and part of speech, the most common definition and one sentence for each word.*

Pronunciations

We've included the most popular pronunciations. Additional pronunciations may exist for some words. We've chosen to use very few special symbols and markings.

Pronunciation Guide:
(a) - as in *sad, tap, latch*
(ā) - as in *a* in *pay, late, cape*
(ä) - as in *father, hot*
(e) - as in *led, set, deck*
(ē) - as in *feel, deal, easy*
(ə) - as in *about, confuse*

(i) - as in *lip, fish*
(ī) - as in *tide, white, ripe*
(ō) - as in *cone, rope, snow*
(u) - as in *sun, umbrella*
(oo) - as in *poodle*
(yoo) - as in *bugle, uniform*

(g) – as in *gum, gorilla*
(t) - any letter inside parenthesis within another syllable may or may not be pronounced.

The main emphasis in each word belongs on the syllable in **bold** type.

1. hackneyed (**hak**-nēd) *Middle English.* adjective: overused, trite
    No one like the new love song because its lyrics were so hackneyed.

2. behemoth (bi-**hē**-muth) *Hebrew.* noun: a very large object or creature
    Grandpa's old truck is a behemoth compared to our compact car.

3. assuage (ə-**swāj**) *Middle English, Old French, Vulgar Latin.* verb: make less severe
    Visits from friends served to assuage the widow's grief.

4. coalesce (kō-ə-**les**) *Latin.* verb: to unite so as to form one whole
    Opposing groups finally decided to coalesce and avoid a civil war.

5. erudite (**er**-yoo-dīt) *Middle English* adjective: learned, scholarly
    The erudite speaker had a difficult time relating to her young audience.

Please note that every effort has been made to ensure the accuracy of all information for each word. Occasionally, sources differ on some items.

6. garrulous (**gar**-ə-ləs) *Latin.* adjective: overly talkative
   The garrulous newcomer soon bored the other guests at the party.

7. harangue (hə-**rang**) *Middle French, Italian.* noun or verb   noun: a long verbal attack or scolding
   The teacher's harangue only served to make the student more nervous.

8. quiescent (kwē-**es**-ənt, kwī-**es**-ənt) *Latin.* adjective: quiet or inactive
   After the high-pressure deal had been made, the relieved executive entered a quiescent state of relaxation.

8. puissant (**pyoo**-ə-sənt) *Middle English, Vulgar Latin.* adjective: powerful, potent
   The puissant speech moved many to join the protest.

9. precocious (pri-**kō**-shəs) *Latin.* adjective: talented beyond one's age
   It was apparent to everyone that the young pianist was quite precocious.

10. adulation (aj-ə-**lā**-shən) *Middle English, Middle French, Latin.* noun: high or excessive praise
    The rock star had become accustomed to cries of adulation at his concerts.

11. ephemeral (i-**fem**-rəl) *Greek.* adjective: momentary, fleeting
    She was saddened that the joys of the day were so ephemeral.

12. psoriasis (sə-**rī**-ə-sis) *Neo-Latin, Greek.* noun: a chronic inflammatory skin disease
    The scaly psoriasis on her scalp became very dry and itchy.

13. camaraderie (käm-**rä**-də-rē) *French.* noun: friendship, comradeship
    The camaraderie among the foursome was as enjoyable as the golf game.

14. milieu (mil-**yoo**) *French* noun: surroundings
    The upperclass neighborhood was a milieu that was both unfamiliar and uncomfortable to him.

15. vignette (vin-**yet**) *French* noun: a small illustration or photograph, a brief scene or essay
    The vignette at the beginning of each chapter captured the mood of the text.

16. deification (dē-ə-fi-**kā**-shən) *Middle English, Late Latin.* noun: the act of exalting to the rank of a god
    The ancient king's success in war led to his deification.

17. querulous (**kwer**-ə-ləs) *Latin.* adjective: irritable, complaining
    The lawyer's querulous tone of voice earned her no favors with the jury.

18. catamaran (kat-ə-mə-**ran**) *Tamil.* noun: a sailboat with two identical hulls
    The catamaran moved swiftly has the wind grew stronger.

19. rancorous (**rang**-ker-əs) *Old French, Late Latin.* adjective: bitter, hateful
    The business partners' rancorous relationship led to the company's downfall.

20. antediluvian (an-tē-də-**loo**-vē-ən) *Latin.* adjective: occurring before the Great Flood
    The antediluvian story of Cain and Abel has always interested me.

21. euphoric (yoo-**for**-ik) *Greek.* adjective: extremely happy or confident
    She was euphoric when she won the spelling bee.

22. solder (**sod**-er) *Middle English, Old French* noun: fusible alloy used to join metals
    John used solder to weld the broken pipe.

23. scythe (sī*th*) *Middle English, Old English* noun: an implement made of a long curved blade fastened to a handle, used to cut grain or grass by hand
    The farmer swung the scythe back and forth across the field, cutting the ripened wheat.

24. dirigible (**dir**-i-jə-bəl) *Latin.* noun: an airship
    The sportscasters broadcast the soccer game from a dirigible.

25. reminiscent (rem-ə-**nis**-ənt) *Latin.* adjective: tending to remind one of something similar; suggestive
    The pine-scented candle is reminiscent of many past Christmas trees.

26. troubadour (**troo**-bə-door) *French.* noun: a wandering singer or minstrel
    Because he could both sing and act, Morgan played the part of a troubadour in the community play.

27. verbiage (**ver**-bē-ij) *French.* noun: an overabundance of words
    There was so much verbiage in the speech that the thirty minute address could have been given in just five minutes.

28. zephyr (**zef**-er) *Middle English, Latin, Greek.* noun: a gentle, light breeze
    Sitting on the porch in the evening, we found the zephyr to be most enjoyable.

29. omniscience (om-**nish**-əns) *Medieval Latin.* noun: infinite knowledge
    The super hero was said to have powers of omniscience and longevity.

30. onomatopoeia (on-ə-mat-ə-**pē**-ə) *Late Latin, Greek.* noun: the formation of a word from a sound associated with what is named, such as *honk, meow* or *sizzle*
    Our assignment was to use alliteration and onomatopoeia in poetry.

* Please note that every effort has been made to ensure the accuracy of all information for each word. Occasionally, sources differ on some items.

✂   ✂   ✂   ✂   ✂   ✂   ✂

THE SPELLING BEE TOOLBOX™
Clip art, Bookmarks, Reminders, Name Tags and Award Certificates

It's Spelling Bee Time!

www.spelling-words-well.com

Spelling Bee Season...

...How sweet it is!

www.spelling-words-well.com

Look Out! The Spelling Bee is coming!

www.spelling-words-well.com

Bee an Expert.

Bee ready for the Bee!

www.spelling-words-well.com

THE SPELLING BEE TOOLBOX ™
Bookmarks

Bookmark 1:

Don't BEE too Busy to study for the BEE!

Words to Study:

_____
_____
_____
_____
_____
_____
_____
_____
_____
_____
_____
_____

www.spelling-words-well.com

Bookmark 2:

15 Fabulous Words to Study:

1. _____
2. _____
3. _____
4. _____
5. _____
6. _____
7. _____
8. _____
9. _____
10. _____
11. _____
12. _____
13. _____
14. _____
15. _____

www.spelling-words-well.com

Bookmark 3:

Bee Prepared

Bee Confident

Bee On Time

Bee a Winner!

www.spelling-words-well.com

Spelling Bee Reminder

Date: _____

Time: _____

Place: _____

Other important info: _____

_____

_____

Don't "Bee" **LATE** for the Bee!

www.spelling-words-well.com

Spelling Bee Reminder

Date: _____

Time: _____

Place: _____

Other important info: _____

_____

_____

Don't Bee Square. Bee There!

www.spelling-words-well.com

THE SPELLING BEE TOOLBOX™
Name Tags – See directions on page 8.

Congratulations

to

_____

Winner of the _____
Spelling Bee

Held on _____, 20____

at

_____

Great Job!

_____   _____
Spelling bee coordinator   Teacher

© 2011 www.spelling-words-well.com

Congratulations

to

_____

for finishing in ____ place
in the _____ Spelling Bee

Held on _____, 20____

at

_____

Great Job!

_____   _____
Spelling bee coordinator   Teacher

© 2011 www.spelling-words-well.com

Congratulations

to

_____

Winner of the _____
Spelling Bee

Held on _____, 20____

at

_____

Great Job!

_____   _____
Spelling bee coordinator   Teacher

© 2011 www.spelling–words–well.com

This award goes to

_____

Winner of the

_____ Spelling Bee

held on _____, 20____

at

_____

Excellent Work!

_____
Principal

_____
Teacher

© 2011 www.spelling-words-well.com

This award goes to

_____

for finishing in _____ place in the

_____ Spelling Bee

held on _____, 20____

at

_____

Nice Job!

_____
Principal

_____
Teacher

© 2011 www.spelling–words–well.com

This award goes to

_____

for your participation in the

_____ Spelling Bee

held on _____, 20____

at

_____

Thanks for being in our Bee!

_____
Principal

_____
Teacher

© 2011 www.spelling-words-well.com

This

Spelling Bee Certificate

is hereby awarded to

_____

WINNER of the

_____ Spelling Bee

held on _____, 20____

at

_____

CONGRATULATIONS!

_____   _____
Principal   Teacher

© 2014 www.spelling-words-well.com

This
Spelling Bee Certificate
is hereby awarded to

_____

____-place finisher of the

_____ Spelling Bee

held on _____, 20____

at

_____

CONGRATULATIONS!

_____   _____
Principal   Teacher

© 2014 www.spelling–words–well.com

This
Spelling Bee Certificate
is hereby awarded to

_____

Participant in the

_____ **Spelling Bee**

held on _____, 20___

at

_____

Nice Work!

_____   _____
Principal   **Teacher**

© 2014 www.spelling-words-well.com

This award goes to

_____

Winner of the

_____ Spelling Bee

held on _____, 20____

at

_____

Your hard work has paid off.
Congratulations!

_____   _____
Principal   Teacher

© 2011 www.spelling–words–well.com

This award goes to

_____

for finishing in _____ place

in the

_____ Spelling Bee

held on _____, 20____

at

_____

Great Work!

_____   _____
Principal   Teacher

© 2011 www.spelling-words-well.com

This award goes to

_____

for your participation in the

_____ Spelling Bee

held on _____, 20____

at

_____

Your participation and hard work
helped to make our spelling bee a success.
Thank you!

_____ _____
Principal   Teacher

© 2011 www.spelling-words-well.com

This is to certify that

_____

was the

WINNER

of the

_____

Spelling Bee

held on _____, 20____

Congratulations!

_____   _____

© 2011 www.spelling-words-well.com

This is to certify that

_____

finished in

_____ place

in the

_____

Spelling Bee

held on _____, 20___

Great Job!

_____   _____

© 2011 www.spelling-words-well.com

This is to certify that

_____

participated in the

_____

Spelling Bee

held on _____, 20___

Thank you for helping to make our bee a success!

_____   _____

© 2011 www.spelling-words-well.com

For more full-color
Spelling Bee Certificates and Name Tags,

please go to:

http://www.spelling-words-well.com/support-files/colored-certificates-gr6-8.pdf

NOTES

NOTES

Thank you for purchasing the

THE SPELLING BEE TOOLBOX™
FOR GRADES 6-8

Also Available: *The Spelling Bee Toolbox for Grades 3-5*

Remember to visit www.spelling-words-well.com for more spelling ideas!
You'll find free worksheets, games, teaching tips, and activities.

You can also find us on Facebook.

About the Author
Ann Richmond Fisher, a former classroom and home school teacher, has been an educational freelance writer for over 25 years. Her innovative books, products and magazine articles have been published by several leading educational publishers. Contact her at spelling.words.well@gmail.com.

Ann is the owner of two websites:
    www.spelling-words-well.com
    www.word-game-world.com

Bryce may be contacted for his web design services through:
https://bryce.fisher-fleig.org/